D1450882

THE CHAMBER MUSIC

OF

JOHANNES BRAHMS

BY

HENRY S. DRINKER, Jr.

GREENWOOD PRESS, PUBLISHERS
WESTPORT, CONNECTICUT

Library of Congress Cataloging in Publication Data

Drinker, Henry Sandwith, 1880-1965.
    The chamber music of Johannes Brahms.

    Bibliography: p.
    1. Brahms, Johannes, 1833-1897. Works,
chamber music. I. Title.
MTL45.B72D8 1974   785.7'0092'4   73-7698
ISBN 0-8371-6941-0

Distributed in 1932 by Elkan-Vogel Co., Philadelphia

Reprinted in 1974 by Greenwood Press,
a division of Williamhouse-Regency Inc.

Library of Congress Catalogue Card Number 73-7698

ISBN 0-8371-6941-0

Printed in the United States of America

CONTENTS.

CONTENTS

ILLUSTRATIONS.

The Chamber Music of Johannes Brahms

FOREWORD

This essay was prepared for the performance in Philadelphia, on the centenary of the birth of Johannes Brahms, of all his works of chamber music. Its purpose is to assist those who study and hear this music to understand it more thoroughly and intimately.

The sketch of Brahms' life and character includes only such events as might reasonably have influenced his music. The analysis of the principal characteristics of his music is given with the full appreciation of the impossibility of demonstration.

Brahms' complete works have been tabulated in groups, so arranged as to enable those wishing to perform them, to see at a glance which are adapted to the performers available.

Following the tabulation is an attempt to point out the technical features of Brahms' music which distinguish it from that of other composers. This has been the most interesting part of the work. It is a subject as to some features of which all will probably agree. As to others, however, one may expect and hope for a delightful and stimulating difference of opinion among persons whose views are the most respected.

For the benefit of those wishing to make a further study of Brahms' life and works, a summary is given of the principal bibliography.

Finally, there is a history and brief discussion of

each of the twenty-four works, in the order of their proposed performance in the present series. The object of this is not to give a musical discussion or analysis of the composition (unnecessary to one who is familiar with it and useless to one who is not) but rather to recreate the atmosphere in which it first appeared, to collect the impressions of the composer's friends and contemporaries, and to point out musical features of especial interest or significance.

Brahms produced his works not by ignoring what his predecessors had accomplished, but by adopting from them all that he believed sound and valuable, consolidating and organizing it for his own purposes. The precedent of the master has been followed here, without, however, the pretence of any such addition as that by which Brahms created music, based on what had gone before, but nevertheless essentially his own. All that could be found of interest in the litera- ture on Brahms, both as to facts and to suggestions, has been ruthlessly extracted and used in the present volume, with and without quotation marks. Since no credit is claimed herein for originality with regard to anything, specific acknowledgment of each appropria- tion is considered unnecessary.

When Brahms published the Hungarian Dances he was careful (in spite of the fact that several of the tunes were his very own) to do so without Opus number and with the designation "Arranged by J. Brahms." Again following the Master, the present essay (which has in no sense been an Opus) has been merely "Ar- ranged by a Philadelphia Disciple."

November 15, 1932.

SKETCH OF BRAHMS' LIFE

When Johannes Brahms was born at Hamburg on May 7th, 1833, Beethoven had been dead for six years, Schubert for five; Mendelssohn was 24, Schumann 23, Liszt 21, Wagner 20. Although Brahms' early youth coincided with the height of Mendelssohn's popularity, the latter's music had no really permanent or important effect on that of Brahms, as did the music of Bach and Beethoven. Nor did the music of Schumann, except perhaps momentarily. The personality of Schumann and that of his wife Clara (Wieck) were, however, the greatest single influence on his career.

Brahms' ancestors "wrested a frugal sustenance from a hostile ocean and a meagre soil." He had no ascertainable musical heredity behind his father, who was a capable bread and butter contra-bass player, like hundreds of others. Although the boy's genius showed itself at an early age (at six he had eagerly invented his own system of musical notation) he was not a precocious wonder-child like Mozart, nor ever exploited as such. At seven his father took him for piano lessons to Otto Cossel, a competent teacher, who three years later turned him over to his own master, Edward Marxen, probably the soundest available musician within the feasible radius of Hamburg. Marxen gave him, without charge, lessons in piano and later in composition. Johannes' progress in both was very rapid. He was an indefatigable worker, with an unquenchable enthusiasm for overcoming difficulties. At ten, we find him playing in

[3]

public the piano part in the Beethoven quintet (Op. 16) for piano and wind, and a Mozart piano quartet. At fourteen he gave a concert of his own, as a virtuoso, and played, in addition to the Beethoven Waldstein sonata, an original "Fantasia on a favorite waltz." The next six years were devoted to the hardest kind of work, both at the piano and in composition, with little school as such, but much reading of many good books, bought second-hand,—earning a little by lessons and by playing at dance halls (with a volume of poetry on the music stand), with sufficient outdoors to build up a body which knew no fatigue, needed but five hours of sleep (obtainable instantly anywhere and at any hour of the day) and which suffered no real illness until that which proved fatal (April 3, 1897, at 64) within less than a year of its inception.

Brahms had heard Joachim (two years his senior) play the Beethoven concerto in Hamburg in 1848, and had heard Schumann conduct his works there in 1850, but did not meet either of them until 1853. During this summer, Brahms went on a concert tour with the Hungarian violinist Remenyi, whose fame rests on his wholly unfounded claim as the real author of the Hungarian Dances and on the fact that it was in the course of this tour that, when the piano at Colle was a half-tone flat, Brahms, without the music, transposed the Beethoven C minor piano-violin sonata to C sharp (he later performed the same feat for Joachim with the Kreutzer sonata). Remenyi was also the sole (and most unreliable) authority for the picturesque story of Brahms having gone to sleep while Liszt was playing to the two young musicians and his other guests at Weimar.

At Hanover Remenyi took Brahms to call on Joachim (a former fellow-student in Vienna) who was so charmed with Brahms' personality and so impressed with the originality and power of the songs and sonatas which the unassuming blond boy played to him with such fire and freedom, that he invited Brahms to visit him in Göttingen at the close of the concert tour. There, during the following two months, was formed the deepest friendship Brahms had with any man. In spite of a coolness after Brahms took the part of Joachim's wife at the time of their divorce, Joachim was always unbounded in his respect and love for his friend's works and did more than anyone to make them known in Europe, as conductor, as soloist in the violin concerto which was written for and dedicated to him, as a partner with Brahms in sonata tours, and as leader of the famous Joachim quartet. For years the two young musicians exchanged each day by mail an exercise in counterpoint or other form of composition, on pain of a cash fine used by the other to buy books. For Joachim's musical opinion, Brahms had also the highest respect, and submitted many of his principal works to him for criticism and suggestion before publication. "There is more in J," he wrote Frau Schumann in 1855, "than in all of us young people put together."

Brahms left Joachim and Göttingen in the middle of August, on foot, armed with Joachim's cards introducing musical friends along the Rhine and with a letter to Robert Schumann at Düsseldorf, at whose home he arrived late in September. Both Schumann and his wife Clara (one of the greatest woman pianists and musicians of all time) were overwhelmed by the genius of his sonatas ("veiled symphonies", Schumann called them) and by his playing of them. Also they immediately fell in love with him and he with them. They made him, as it were, a member of the family, and the following month, after Brahms had returned to Hanover with Joachim, Schumann published in the leading musical journal of Germany his famous article entitled "New Paths", in which he hailed Brahms as "him that should come, bringing mastership, not in process of development, but springing forth, like Minerva, fully armed from the head of Jove". Citing piano-sonatas, songs, quartets for strings, violin sonatas "every one so different from the rest that each seemed to flow from a separate source" he predicted even greater things when this "highest genius" will "sink his magic staff in masses of chorus and orchestra."

The modern psychologist will shudder at the danger to this modest, ingenuous boy, with his long fair hair and his still high-pitched voice, when thus catapulted from utter obscurity into the veriest spot-light of the musical stage. "Before he had well begun to climb the steep hill of reputation, he found himself transported to its summit." But this boy's character was too strong, his independence too assured and his artistic ideals too unassailable to be harmed or upset even by premature success. "Neither severe criticism nor unbounded approval turned him from the straight road to the goal he had before him, nor hindered him from striving as he went to conquer all his besetting faults."

Schumann's article probably made, for the time at least, as many sceptics as friends. Liszt wrote to Bülow (who 25 years later became Brahms' loudest and, next to Joachim and Clara Schumann, his most effective supporter—he invented the phrases "The Three Bs" and "The Tenth Symphony") that the article was costing him no sleep, as Schumann had said much the same thing fifteen years before of the genius of Sterndale Bennett.

Brahms wrote Schumann that the public praise thus bestowed "obliges me above all to take the greatest care in the selection of what is to be published." In spite of the flattering offers of the publishers who "offered me all the money which I as a poor young man had much difficulty in earning", he gave them at the time only the two piano sonatas Op. 1 and 2, the songs Op. 3, and the scherzo Op. 4, and did not include "either of my trios", a string quartet in B flat, a duet for piano and cello, numerous "sarabandes, gavottes and gigues," or the "fantasia on a popular waltz". A violin sonata in A minor was to be Op. 5, but was lost by Liszt and Remenyi. During the next twelve months he published the F minor piano sonata Op. 5, the songs Op. 6 and 7, and the B major trio, Op. 8, and then nothing more for six years except the Schumann variations Op. 9 and the Ballades for piano Op. 10, devoting himself wholly to study of the masters and to incessant practice in every form of musical gymnastics, including canons and fugues by the score, in every conceivable form.

His bedroom was at one time papered with his songs and with discarded string quartets. "Better", he said "that I should take them down and burn them than another."

This remarkable poise and self-restraint is one of his most important characteristics. His ability to criticize his own work impersonally was marred only by his false notion that the excellence of a musical phrase or idea may best be tested by whether or not it returns of itself to the composer's mind a second time after being dismissed when first conceived. This notion, in which he persisted to the end, doubtless led Brahms to lose forever many subtle ideas which Beethoven would have noted down, and also, perhaps, to develop some which might better have been replaced by those thus forgotten.

Brahms' personal relations with Robert Schumann, though so important a factor in his career and development, were short-lived. Within five months Schumann's mental malady brought on an attempted suicide, after which he was placed in a private asylum, where he died two years later. During almost all this period, Brahms practically lived at the Schumann house, managing the household and caring for the children during the concert tours which Frau Schumann was forced to undertake to support her family, and comforting and strengthening her during her brief home comings. The relation which developed between them is extraordinary and anomalous. She was fourteen years his senior, the mother of seven young children, and the wife and later the widow of his beloved master, benefactor and friend. No one can read their beautiful letters to each other without being certain both that this was no platonic love, no merely maternal or filial affection, and in spite of this that their relation was very noble and beautiful. Frau Schumann, without abating any of her devotion to her husband, was swept away by this impetuous young demi-god, whose genius she almost worshipped. Brahms had for her musicianship the deepest respect and for her personality an adoration which effectively walled him off from the normal love and marriage that otherwise might have been his. Apparently there came a time when he concluded that his life's work would go on better if he tore himself from this relationship, and he did so, though it left a scar in his soul that never healed.

After this he had several rather mild affairs (not to mention Julie Schumann, who was probably a mere overtone of her mother) but he never went on with them, either because at the time he did not consider himself in a condition to marry, or, perhaps, because he dreaded being "guided" through life. He did not want to be guided nor to be too much sympathized with. While he fully appreciated the charm of women—"only women do everything quickly and well at the same time", he wrote Clara Schumann when 21—and while he craved the close companionship which only marriage and children could bring, he was always unwilling to risk the sacrifice of his independence and deliberately chose to be "free though lonely."

From 1857 to 1859, Brahms spent his early winters at Detmold, where he was Director of the Choral Society for the local Prince, and had, besides, the small orchestra to work with, as well as much chamber-music. There and at Hamburg during this period and the three following years, he finished the two serenades (Op. 11 and 16), the D minor piano concerto (Op. 15), the B flat sextet (Op. 18), and the two piano quartets (Op. 25 and 26), as well as several works for womens' voices written for his "Ladies Chorus" at Hamburg. This "Ladies Chorus" was one of the happiest events of his life.

The very hostile reception of the Concerto at the initial performance in Leipsic in January, 1859, did not in the least shake his confidence, either in the composition or in his ultimate success.

Brahms' public recognition as a great composer really began with his first pilgrimage to Vienna, where, in September of 1862, he went with his two piano quartets, his new piano variations (Op. 21, 23 and 24), the two serenades, and particularly with the Bb sextet. His determination to take this trip followed his deep chagrin at being passed over for conductor of the Orchestra and Choral Society at his native city Hamburg, which he much coveted, and denial of which he did not quite forgive even when given the freedom of the City twenty-seven years later. From 1862 on, his reputation steadily grew until, beginning with the performance of the Requiem all over Germany in 1868–9, he was recognized by all but a few scoffers as the leader of living composers of absolute music.

After the notable performance of the Requiem in the Bremen Cathedral, Clara Schumann, who, with all Brahms' nearest friends, had come for the occasion, wrote in her diary:

"Good Friday, April 10th, 1868. The Requiem has taken hold of me as no sacred music ever did before. As I saw Johannes standing there, baton in hand, I could not help thinking of my dear Robert's prophecy, 'Let him but only grasp the magic wand and work with orchestra and chorus,' which is fulfilled today."

It was not with Brahms' assent or approval that he was hailed by the anti-Wagner faction as their champion, in the controversy which raged during the last half of the 19th Century. Brahms was never actively anti-Wagner, but merely pro-Brahms. He was always most scrupulous in refraining from anything which might be interpreted as hostile to Wagner, or as belittling Wagner's music, and never stooped to reply or to pay any attention to the many venemous attacks which were launched at him by Wagner, who referred to him as the "wooden Johannes" and permitted the Bayreuther Blätter to call him the "Eunuch of Music". Indeed, Brahms' complacent dignity seemed to infuriate Wagner the more. Brahms sincerely respected Wagner as a musician, realized fully his tremendous influence on the music of his time, was intimately familiar with his scores, and frequently attended performances of Wagner's later works in Vienna. Recognizing that there was room in the artistic world both for him and for Wagner, he did not believe in Wagner's theory of the music-drama, or in the possibility of continuous music which would continue to be music. While Brahms fully appreciated the function of music to supplement an emotional state, as in a love-song, a requiem, a battle song or

a song of triumph, and occasionally put in a bit of
realism (like the church-bells in Maria's Kirchgang,
Op. 22, or the nightingale in No. 1 of Op. 92) he did
not believe it possible to make a musical phrase
represent a physical fact, or a character or a phase
of one.

Nor did he really like Wagner's music, though
he did his best to understand and to appreciate it.
In spite of the efforts of Specht and Widmann to
make us believe that he did, a letter to Clara Schumann after a performance of the Meistersinger, and
one from Joachim to the latter's wife after he and
Brahms had been to hear Rheingold, would seem to
give us the truth:

> "I am not," Brahms writes (in answer to
> Frau Schumann's request for a candid opinion
> of the Meistersinger "not as to an anti-Wagner-
> ite") "enthusiastic myself—either about this work
> or about Wagner in general. But I listen to it
> as attentively as possible and as often—as I can
> stand it. It is certainly a subject that lends
> itself to discussion. All the same, I am glad that
> I have not got to say all I think quite clearly
> and loudly, etc. etc."

> "The Rheingold", Joachim writes to Amalie,
> "did not teach me anything new about Wagner;
> it is really almost boring with its eternal mystery
> and elaboration. Even Brahms was forced to
> agree with me, although he likes to pose as an
> admirer of Wagner."

The nearest Brahms came to drama with music
was Rinaldo, which is not one of his great works.
For a long time he searched, or let himself believe

that he was searching, in vain for a suitable operatic
text. We may perhaps be thankful that he was unable to find one with which he was satisfied, since
this, coupled with his comparatively mild success as
a pianist and conductor, allowed him to concentrate
all his interest, energy and power on the production
of absolute music.

In the winter of 1863–4, as conductor of the
Vienna Singacademie, and during the three seasons
of 1872–1875, as "Artistic Director" of the Vienna
Gesellschaft der Musikfreunde, Brahms occupied his
final regular positions as conductor. In the fall of
1871 he moved permanently to Vienna, where for his
last twenty-five years the genial, care-free people,—
typified by the waltzes of Johann Strauss in which
Brahms never ceased to delight—, furnished the
environment to supplement his bleak northern heredity.
The greater part of his important compositions were
completed during his long summer "vacations" spent
in the country. "The few notes which I write during
the winter" he once told Heuberger, "are of absolutely
no importance." At Lichtenthal, near Clara Schumann, from 1864 to 1872, at Portschach (1877–1880),
Murzschlag in Styria (1884–1885), Thun (1886–1888),
Ischl (1880, 1882, 1889–1896) and other beautiful
places for single seasons, working at his desk in the
morning, walks in the woods and fields during the
afternoon, the evenings with his many friends, music
and talk. His winters were largely taken up with
concert tours at which he conducted his works with
various orchestras and choruses. (Joachim says that
when he came out to bow to the audience, his action

was like that of a swimmer who comes to the surface
and shakes the water from his hair). He frequently
played the piano part of his chamber music both in
public and at the homes of his friends.

One year was much like another, except for the
astounding variety of the works produced, each of
which, however, was the result of much thought and
often of repeated revision. The first two string
quartets (Op. 51) were published in 1873, after (as he
told Widmann) twenty previous attempts at this form
had been completed and destroyed as unsatisfactory.
The First Symphony (Op. 68) was first performed in
November, 1876, although the beginning of the allegro
from the first movement is quoted by Clara Schumann
in a letter to Joachim dated July 1, 1862, telling of
Johannes "growing Symphony"; the body of the last
movement dates back to the early fifties. The well
known theme in C major, given out by the French
horn in the introduction to the last movement, and
by some critics traced to the Westminster chimes, was
sent by Brahms to Frau Schumann from Switzerland
on a post card for her birthday, September 13, 1868,
with the words "Thus blew the shepherds horn today"
and to go with the music:

"Hoch auf'm Berg, tief im Thal,
Grüz ich dich viel tausend-mal!"

Although in his early years a remarkable pianist,
in later years Brahms apparently became careless in
his technique. Clara tells in her diary how, on one
occasion, she and Joachim exchanged horrified glances
at his performance of the Schumann E flat piano

quartet, and Ferdinand Schumann relates how his grandmother protested to the family at his performance of the clarinet sonatas in public. In her diary we also find the following amusing entries:—

> (May 24, 1854) "It is not easy to play with Brahms [four hands]. He plays too arbitrarily and cares nothing for a crochet more or less."
> (December 29, 1882) "The pity is that Brahms plays more and more abominally,—it is now nothing but thump, bang and scrabble."

Despite these outbursts (she always was outraged at her idol's occasional lapses from perfection), when Brahms was in the right mood and had a thoroughly sympathetic and intelligent audience, he could do things with the piano possible only for a great master of the instrument. Indeed, his instrumentation started from the piano and worked toward the other instruments. We may wish to have been at Hanover one summer evening, when Brahms and Joachim played the three violin sonatas for the King and Queen, or to have heard from his own hands "the confidential Brahms of the chamber music" at Frau Schumann's house in Frankfurt, when he brought Joachim and Hausmann and Mühlfeld to play to her his latest trio or sonata.

Except for frequent vacation trips to Italy, where he loved the sunny country, the easy going people and the works of art, he could never be induced to journey far from home. He refused the offered degree from Cambridge University because of the trip and the formalities involved. Apparently he never crossed the

French border, and not even for a moment considered a tour in the United States, in spite of the early recognition here of his works, chiefly through the efforts of William Mason, (who had met him at Liszt's house in Weimar in 1853) and those of his intimate friend Henschel, the first conductor of the Boston Orchestra. Everywhere that he went, however, he was universally recognized and respected, despite the carpings of the "New German" clique, who aimed to create poetry and painting in tones instead of making music. Indeed, the last fifteen years of his life were as replete with honors as any artist could desire. "You are honored," Clara Schumann wrote in 1894, "in every land, and it goes on and on. What a magnificent feeling it must be for you." Typical of his relations with the world was his status at Meiningen where after his introduction in 1881 by Bülow to the music loving Duke, he was a frequent guest, royally entertained, and where the fine orchestra and chorus, first under Bülow and then Fritz Steinbach, were always at his disposal to try his new works.

At the three day music festival in Meiningen in October, 1895, works by Bach, Beethoven and Brahms only were heard. Brahms, as Joachim wrote Clara Schumann, "was honored as one of the Immortals." "He is indeed to be envied and not the least because he can say that he has not falsified the prophecies of his noble predecessor among our masters."

THE MAN AND HIS MUSIC

In appearance Brahms was a typical Teuton. His straight sandy hair came nearly down to his shoulders; his light blue eyes, softened by fair eyelashes "were wonderfully keen and bright with now and then a roguish twinkle in them, and yet at times of almost childlike tenderness." It was not until 1878 that he permanently grew a beard. (He fooled all his friends on his first temporary appearance with it in 1866, introducing himself as "Kappellmeister Muller from Brunswick".) Although careless in dress, regarding comfort solely and convention not at all, his linen was always spotlessly clean. When his trousers were too long for comfort, he cut them off with the scissors above his shoetops; on a cold day, he wore three pair, one over the other. Black coffee and strong cigars were his two inseparables. His figure was rather short and square (tending later to stoutness), with a broad chest and herculean shoulders, a healthy, ruddy complexion indicative of out-doors, a thick and protruding though genial underlip, and a powerful head, which he threw back energetically when playing. "In his countenance," says Widmann, "there lay the promise of victory, the radiating cheerfulness of a mind revelling in the exercise of its power". "His mind," said Joachim of him at 21, "is capable of grasping the sublimest as well as the tenderest conceptions". "It did not, however, require the tragically sublime to move him deeply; pure beauty, if ever so simply expressed, could do this."

The dominating trait in Brahms' character was the utter purity and singleness of purpose with which he pursued his artistic ideals. Although certain from the beginning that public approval would eventually come, and although often irritated at its absence, the recognition that he looked for was not of the greatness of Brahms, but of the music which he knew himself capable of producing. "He will not" wrote Joachim in 1854, "make the smallest sacrifice of his intellectual inclinations". No approval thus secured would have in the least satisfied him.

If thus relentlessly to pursue a constantly mounting artistic ideal, impelled by a noble passion for perfection, is egotism, Brahms was supremely egotistic. As Robert Schumann wrote of him to Joachim, however, after his first visit, "although always on the lookout for something to his own advantage, * * * anything he does seize is only used to help him in his efforts to become a great artist—that is saying much, when one compares him with others."

It is, of course, apparent from his letters and from the accounts of his behaviour by his contemporaries, that he very often allowed his own purity of purpose, his abhorrence of all that smacked of sham, his obsession for independence, and his delight in squelching pomposity, to make him unjustly oblivious or even cruelly scornful of the motives and merits of many worthy people. "His ruggedness", says Eugenie Schumann in her Memoirs, "was in a perpetual state of defense against suspected attacks by others on his independence and the privacy of his existence." "He simply could not endure people", says Heuberger "who showed that they were running after him." Much of his apparent brusqueness and roughness of manner was, however, due merely to his constitutional want of presence of mind in trifling matters and to the kind of stubborn shyness which hides deep feeling behind a wholly inappropriate rebuff or jest. At heart he was as pure and simple as the children and animals whom he loved and who loved him; without envy or arrogance, and free from all taint of the meaner emotions. "Pure as a diamond, soft as snow", Joachim said of him. While in his later years he allowed his admirers to turn him into a social tryant, he would have none around him who were merely lion-hunters, but only those who had for him and for whom he entertained a real regard. "He had to the last the power of attracting the abiding love of loyal friends."

In 1858 Brahms wrote to Clara Schumann:—

"All of you, particularly you, think me different from what I am. I am never, or very seldom, in the least bit pleased with myself. I never feel quite happy, but fluctuate between complacency and depression."

In his later years he said to his friend, Rudolf von the Leyen:—

"Those who meet me in company where I seem contented and ready to jest with others, must think me cheerful; to you, I need hardly say that within myself I never laugh."

Specht thinks that this was the result of his relations with "Klara," "the only woman whom I ever really loved". It would seem more likely that it followed from his ingrowing nature, which would never allow him freely to open his sore heart to anyone. He seemed at times to take a morbid delight in hurting those whom he loved best. The demon in him he loosened against the very persons in whose affection he felt the most secure. Eugenie Schumann tells how she and her sisters used to suffer at the way he used frequently and deliberately to wound the feelings of their mother, whose great heart could never understand this. "I am sure", says Eugenie, "that Brahms suffered more than he made others suffer by his faults." He was almost always the one, however, to make the first move to a reconciliation, and Frau Schumann's big warm soul was always ready to meet him more than half-way. Strange it is that his music did not seem to give him a sufficient outlet to effect serenity. In the later years, perhaps it did.

Brahms' truly kindly and very lovable self, as well as his courage and independence and his faith in the inherent goodness of things are all epitomized in a letter which he wrote Frau Schumann on her postponement, (because of an accident to her hand at the Tiergarten) of a visit to him at Vienna:—

                                        "Vienna,
                                        March 6, 1865.
"DEAREST CLARA

"I send as big a sigh as that to begin with!
"I half expected it, although I have been spending all these days getting my room tidy,

and trying to make everything nice—I had ordered new coffee-cups, had the plate cleaned and bought fire-works! preserves! in short had done all that impatience and loving expectation could do The lateness of the season is the chief thing which makes me say yes to your decision.

"I have at once cancelled the engagements and countermanded the rooms, but I cannot so quickly and easily cancel my own hopes.

"Above all things, I hope that you will take the matter, as a whole and in detail, not in the spirit befitting a Christian who has to regard all crosses great and small as luxury, but as becomes a human being who (like yourself) has always done her duty, and who has a right to expect something from Providence—and who, after all, did not lay out the Tiergarten, and is in no wise responsible for this misfortune.

"I know that it is easy to preach, but you must not let your heart be weighed down by the cares of this world—and as to the other you have no need to be anxious——

"I should be sincerely glad to hear that you had simply drawn a thick line through this winter in your book of receipts, that you do not allow any little blue devils to argue, and that you think of bracing yourself with all sorts of edifying things, such as philosophy. The world is round and it must turn; what God does is well done; consider the lilies, etc., or better still, do not think at all, for things cannot be altered, and a wise man repents of nothing. And so the word is simply 'forward'; keep your head erect and let none but beautiful and happy thoughts find a home in it, as befits a 'splendid specimen of humanity' " * * *

"You see everything so warmly with such beautiful serenity, first, like a reflection of yourself; and then, with the same serenity, you give unto each his due . ."

Brahms' purity of artistic purpose is reflected throughout his music. From the thundering opening of the C major Sonata (Op. 1) through the last of the Vier Ernste Gesange (Op. 121), there is not a note designed merely to please the audience, without contributing to the expression or development of the musical idea. Brahms never "showed off". His is the rugged plain-speaking which in art, as in individuals, is so often misunderstood. He never stooped to tickle the public ear with amiable babbling. "I have" he wrote to Clara Schumann "a perfect terror of all that smacks of Liszt." (This despite his expressed conviction that Liszt was the greatest pianist of them all).

He cared little for that rapid passing from color to color that constitutes so much of the charm of modern music. His aversion to everything that fascinates by merely external or transient attraction eliminated from his music all that is trite and commonplace. That part of the public which is accustomed to having its artistic food specially prepared and predigested has therefore considered his music "obscure", whereas it is merely difficult to grasp quickly. "Obscurity" implies either a vagueness of idea or a lack of skill in expressing it, whereas the failure to understand Brahms at first hearing results from unfamiliarity with his idiom and from the fact that his musical ideas are so weighty and often so complex that they cannot be expressed in language of infantile simplicity. In 1799 a Vienna critic wrote of the three Beethoven Sonatas, Op. 10:—

"Mr. van Beethoven goes his own path, and a dreary, eccentric and tiresome path it is, learning, learning, and nothing but learning, but not a bit of nature or melody".

Brahms' music is wholly self-reliant. Its strength lies in the importance of the musical ideas themselves, and in the soundness of their relation to one another, and not in a startling method of presenting them, or in any relation between them and non-musical ideas. His music is architectural rather than pictorial. Those persons will never understand or like Brahms who require labels,—titles and sub-titles—for everything, and who lean always on the imagination of others. While Brahms fully understood the proper function of music to supplement an emotional state, and used music in this way with supreme skill and understanding in his songs and choral works, his absolute music is music and nothing else. The learned German biographers who labor to discover in his orchestral, chamber and piano works hidden allusions to events in his life not only have wasted their time but have misled many of their readers. Thus Kalbeck's theory that the opening of the D Minor Concerto describes poor half-crazed Schumann leaping off the Rhine bridge at Dusseldorf, is too absurd for discussion. This Concerto is merely the music which burst from Brahms at the age of twenty-three, when he was overflowing with physical and mental vigor, teeming with musical ideas, and boiling with emotional turmoil as a result of the catastrophe to his beloved friend and of his adoration of "dearest Klara."

Almost equally unconvincing are some of the theories of Niemann and Specht as to certain cryptic allusions to his various mild love affairs. For Brahms, art was far too sacred a matter to permit any foolish attempt at story telling. The Clarinet trio (1891, aet. 58) does not, as Specht asserts, "sing but of love alone," nor is the Clarinet quintet, as Miss May and Niemann would have us believe a "retrospect" filled with "resignation" and "loving regret" that the "evening is not far away when no man can work". It is merely the music that Brahms was interested in writing after he had heard Mühlfeld, a "stupendous fellow", play the clarinet, and realized the possibilities of the instrument in combination with strings. These critics forget that Brahms was much more interested in music than in any woman or event or person, including himself. Nor do they apparently realize how the sacred frenzy of creation (which Specht describes so vividly pp. 306-7) will transcend the unimportant circumstances which may have started it. Brahms himself told Henschel that in his young days "the best songs came into my head while brushing my shoes before dawn". While it is interesting to know, from his statement to Dietrich, that the opening theme of the Horn Trio occurred to him as he emerged into the sunlight from the wooded heights above Baden, this theme is not meant at all to describe sunshine or fir trees or anything tangible, but is merely the musical idea to which that environment happened to contribute, and which was developed and perfected at his desk at home. The same idea might just as well have followed welcome news that a sick friend was on the way to recovery, a pleasant word from a beautiful girl, or a satisfactory breakfast.

The German Requiem was much more than a mere lament for Brahms' beloved old mother. A large part of it was undoubtedly written during the months following her death in February, 1865, and while the 5th number was for her, the sketches dated from 1861, and the second movement, the Funeral March, was adapted from the third movement (in C Minor) of an unpublished Symphony written in 1854 and then turned into an unpublished piece for two pianos.

The utter futility of attempting to attribute to Brahms' absolute music a meaning related to external events or even to specific human emotions, is demonstrated by parallelling the analyses by Niemann and Specht of the last part of the F Minor Piano Quintet:

NIEMANN

SPECHT

The *"sinister wrestling* and *sombre* piano quintet" (115) "mighty and *wrathful"* * * * "whose *darkness* is lightened only by the *melancholy* and yet inwardly steadfast andante" (118). "Born of *defiant melancholy* (215) it belongs to the *gloomiest* and greatest music Brahms has ever written" (216)

The finale * * * in spite of the minor key * * * is *thoroughly contented and jovial,* inclined to all sorts of *amusing* little rhythmical *tricks;* and *altogether sportively disposed.*

The introduction to the finale * * * leads to a rondo which takes its ease and yet *seems to find no comfort.* Restless semiquavers in thirds, succeeded by quavers, pulsate through it, the whole is *relentlessly* whipped onward by syncopation; the curiously songless, exclamatory second subject, with its jerking up-beat *brings no ray of light* into the movement;

The *coda* * * * goes *laughing* by till it is finally concentrated still more drastically by means of syncopations. Yet all this does not succeed in checking its *joyful mood;* and, in the concluding lines, it takes its leave by breaking off abruptly as though with *bright ringing laughter.*

The end of the piano quintet is as spacious and *serene* as its opening is grave and full of pathos (289).

The extensive *coda* where the themes, dissolved into a more and more precipitate triplet motion, chase each other in the manner of a stretto, *dashes toward the dark unknown. The composer's heart must have been desolate indeed when he wrote this study in black* (217)

"Painfully born of the composer's soul" (273) with its "atmosphere of exalted joylessness." (276).

While it is often interesting for one intelligent listener to describe to another the picture, story or other tangible impression which a piece of absolute music suggests to him, recognizing that that suggested by the same music to another may be quite different, it is wholly another thing thus complaisantly to assume that the composer had this particular program in mind, or anything like it.

Another distinguishing quality of Brahms' music is self-restraint, which has often been misinterpreted as lack of spontaneity. It is true that Brahms never tears passion to tatters as does Tschaikowsky, nor indulges in an emotional orgy like Tristan, but this does not indicate either lack of spontaneity or that "the craftsman has overshadowed the artist". Much of Brahms' music is as spontaneous as Schubert ("How lovely" in the Requiem, for instance), as inevitable as Beethoven:

> "Es klang so alt und war so neu,
> Wie Vogelsang in süssen Mai."

Simplicity in art is of two kinds, inherent simplicity, like that of the child or the spring-song of the thrush, and simplicity by elimination. Homer, Giotto, Haydn are of the first type, while Shakespeare, Michelangelo, Rodin and Brahms are of the second. The first requires genius, the second both genius, consummate art and self-restraint. The simplicity of much of Brahms' music is appreciated only after repeated hearing when one can realize how much has been said with so few notes or phrases, and how much superfluity has been left out, as with a penstroke in a Rembrandt drawing, or in the last four lines of the Sonnet on Chapman's Homer. Folk-songs, which were Brahms' constant joy and inspiration, are of this second type, constituting what is left after the discard of the unfit and non-essential through many generations. Brahms' music is, as a whole, more compact in form than that of any other composer.

Another reason why Brahms' music is not easily understood, even by the elect, is that its strength often lies not so much in the beauty of one idea as in the relation of several ideas to one another. No aesthetic satisfaction can exceed a joy such as that experienced on the realization that two beautiful themes (like those in the first movement of the D minor violin sonata or in the adagio of the Horn Trio, or in the first and last movements of the B flat string quartet) which, when first heard seem wholly self-sufficient, later are brought together to constitute, in combination, an entirely new musical idea. Those who have intelligently been through this experience will never again decry counterpoint, in the hands of a genius, as a dry and unemotional scientific instrument.

It is this quality in Brahms' music, the presence of so many interesting musical ideas at once,—the richness of his linings,—that makes it both difficult to grasp at first, but of enduring interest. There is no other music which, as a whole, will stand two-piano arrangement for four or eight hands as will that of Brahms. Every player has something important to say on every page. Let any pianist who thinks him-

self entirely familiar with the piano quintet, or with
any of the three piano quartets, try the two-piano
arrangement, and he will at once find beauties, from
the string parts, which he never knew were there.
Wagner made it comparatively easy to follow his
polyphony, first by labelling his motifs—to recognize
them is a sort of game with many Wagnerites, entirely
apart from the music,—and also by repeating them so
many times, though with marvellous variety, that they
cannot fail to be recognized.

The very prevalence, in our time, of the craze
for features, for one tangible idea which can be grasped
and held on to, makes it more difficult for the public
to understand music whose strength lies not so much
in any one feature as in the combination of many.

Brahms was not a great innovator, in spite of
the fact that no composer began with such strength,
originality and daring assertiveness as are found in
the Piano Sonatas, the E flat Minor Scherzo and
the B Major Trio. (In 1853 Berlioz wrote to thank
Joachim for introducing to him "this diffident, auda-
cious young man who has taken into his head to make
a new music").   Brahms began, however, not by
repudiating everything that had gone before, but by
recognizing all that was sound in what his predecessors had discovered and developed. Even in his early
works "the impetuosity of the Minnesinger in him
is allied to the formative organizing power of the
great cathedral builder".

Although Brahms drew freely, from all available
sources, for style and the method of expression,—the
depth and polyphony of Bach, the serenity of Haydn,

the grace of Mozart, the power of Beethoven, the spontaneity of Schubert and the romance of Schumann,—he copied or imitated none of them, any more than Shakespeare copied Virgil or Boccaccio. He was enabled, however, by the tireless training to which he subjected his fertile and many-sided genius, "to couch romantic feeling in classic form", and to discover "how the rugged melodic outlines, the bold harmonic progressions and the large-spanned phrases of modern musical thought, could be organized and brought into that unity in variety which is called beauty". Recognizing the wayward beauties of romanticism, he studied and discovered how to "make them ancillary to that order and fair proportion which is the soul of music". All of his works have both balance and unity.

While Brahms thus became a supreme master of form, he never (some of his critics to the contrary notwithstanding) used form as an end in itself, but only as a means of organizing his teeming ideas into an artistic unit. The disregard of form in art is usually the result either of laziness or of the lack of sufficient mentality and application to master it. Like anarchy it results only in chaos. "Those who make the most diligent search for new forms in music or for new structural possibilities, are usually precisely those in whom the fountain of actual invention runs most slowly". Joachim put it tersely in his address at the Meiningen ceremony after Brahms' death:—

> "For him who dominates all its resources, form is no binding fetter, but a spur, an incentive to new free designs that are preeminently his own."

In 1853, Robert Schumann, who instantly recognized that this boy had in him the future achievement
of all that he himself had been striving for, wrote thus
of the "young eagle" to Joachim:—

> "Johannes is the true apostle, and he will
> write Revelations the secret of which many
> Pharisees will still be unable to unravel even
> centuries later."

More and more, as his idiom becomes familiar,
the greatness and beauty of Brahms' music is receiving
continually wider recognition. Of no other composer,
unless it be Bach, can it be said that his works were
at no previous date more popular than they are today.
Brahms never has been nor will be a mere temporary
enthusiasm. With the public, as with individuals, he
is rarely loved at first sight, but gradually more and
more as he is thoroughly known and studied. Those
who still do not enjoy him may reflect on what a wise
critic wrote at the first hearing of Beethoven's Fifth
Symphony:—

> "I felt that there was a door that was closed
> to me but that behind that door mighty things
> were happening."

Comparatively few people realize the great wealth
and variety of Brahms' contribution to enduring music.
While the four symphonies and the Haydn variations
are now all found on the printed list receiving the high
votes for the request programs, while the violin
concerto and the two piano concertos are in every
repertoire, and while the other orchestral works (the

double concerto, the two overtures and the two serenades) are gradually becoming known, many of the choral works, much of the chamber and piano music, hosts of the solo songs, and practically all of the vocal duets, quartets and motets for four, six and eight voices, are wholly unknown except to a few enthusiasts. Persons who should be wise enough to know tell us that certain of the latter are "abstruse", "dull" and interesting only to the technician. The same was said fifty years ago by critics, equally wise, of the violin concerto, of the fourth symphony, the D Minor Concerto and the F Minor Quintet. May not the modern critics be as wrong as their predecessors, and may it not be well worth while to give more attention to these little known works, in the hope and expectation that, unless they were worthy of him, Brahms would never have left them for us?

TABULATION OF BRAHMS' MUSIC

Brahms' works comprise:

Orchestral: The four Symphonies (Op. 68, 73, 90, 98) Haydn Variations (Op. 56); Two Serenades (Op. 11, 16) Two Overtures (Academic Fest, Op. 80, Tragic, Op. 81) Two Piano Concertos (D minor Op. 15, B flat major, op. 83); Violin Concerto (Op. 77); Double Concerto for Violin and Cello (Op. 102).

Mixed Chorus with Orchestra: German Requiem (Op. 45); Schicksalslied (Op. 54); Triumphlied— eight parts (Op. 55); Nanie (Op. 82); Gesang der Parzen—six parts (Op. 89); Begrabnisgesang (Op. 13, wind instruments only).

Mixed Chorus with Piano: (all above are arranged with piano) Geistliches Lied (Op. 30, organ); 3 songs (six parts, Op. 42 piano ad lib); Tafellied (six parts, Op. 93b); 14 German folk-songs (no Op. number).

Mixed Chrous a capella: 7 Marienlieder (Op. 22); Two motets (six parts, 2 alto, 2 bass, Op. 29); Seven choral songs (2 alto 2 bass, Op. 62); Two motets (four numbers, two of which have two alto and two bass, Op. 74); six songs and Romances (Op. 93a); five songs (three with two alto and two bass, one with two bass, one four part, Op. 104) Fest und Gedenksprecke (eight parts, Op. 109); three motets (four and eight parts, Op. 110).

Mens Chorus and Orchestra: (piano arrangement) Rinaldo, Op. 50, (tenor solo); Alto Rhapsodie, Op. 53 (alto solo).

Mens Chorus a capella: Five Songs (Op. 41).

Womens Chorus and Orchestra: (piano arrangement) Ave Maria—three parts (Op. 12); Four songs (Op. 17 three parts, with two horns and harp). Schubert's Ellens zweiter Gesang (three parts) with four horns and two bassoons (arranged by Brahms).

Womens Chorus with Piano: Psalm XIII (Op. 27, organ); twelve Songs and Romances (Op. 44, piano ad lib).

Womens Chorus a capella: Three Sacred Choruses (Op. 37); Thirteen Canons (three, four and six parts, Op. 113).

52 Solo Vocal Quartets with piano: Op. 31, 64, 92, 112; Op. 52 (Liebeslieder), Op. 65 (Neue Liebslieder), Op. 103, (Gypsy Songs).

31 Vocal Duets with piano: Op. 20, three for soprano and alto; Op. 28, four for alto and baritone; Op. 61, four for soprano and alto; Op. 66, five for soprano and alto; Op. 75, four for "two voices" (alto and tenor, soprano and alto, soprano and tenor, two sopranos); Op. 84, five for "one or two voices"; Op. 52, Nos. 3 and 14, tenor and bass; Nos. 4 and 13, soprano and alto; Op. 65, No. 4, tenor and bass, No. 13, soprano and alto; accompaniments, from figured bass, to Handel duets for women's voices, (no Op. number).

195 Songs (published in four volumes for high and for low voice) for solo voice with piano (16 for baritone, Op. 86, 94, 105; four for bass, Op. 121); two songs for alto with viola obligato, Op. 91; also eight songs in the Liebeslieder Series, Op. 52

and 65, for specific voices; 205 songs in all; also
six books containing German folk-songs and
fourteen children's folk-songs, with original piano
accompaniment.

Chamber Music with Piano: (published in miniature
bound volume); Three violin sonatas (Op. 78,
100, 108); two cello sonatas (Op. 38, 99); two
clarinet sonatas (Op. 120, Nos. 1 and 2); three
trios with violin and cello (Op. 8, original and
revised version; Op. 87, Op. 101); Trio with
violin and french horn, Op. 40; Trio with clarinet
and cello, Op. 114; three piano quartets (Op. 25,
26 and 60); piano quintet, Op. 34; scherzo from
early violin sonata (C Minor).

Chamber Music without piano: (published in miniature
bound volume); Three string quartets (Op. 51
Nos. 1 and 2; Op. 67); two string quintets (two
violas, Op. 88 and 111); two string sextets (Op. 18
and 36); quintet for clarinet and string quartet
(Op. 115).

Piano Music for two hands: (published in two volumes
except Op. 35); Three sonatas, (Op. 1, 2 and 5);
Scherzo, Op. 4; 93 variations and a fugue on 5
themes (Op. 9, Op. 21, Nos. 1 and 2, Op. 24,
Op. 35); 35 other piano pieces (5 Ballades, 18
Intermezzi, 7 Capriccios, 3 Rhapsodies, 1 Romance
Op. 10, 76, 79, 116, 117, 118, and 119; Gavotte
of Gluck, (without Op. number), 5 Studies and
51 exercises without Op. numbers.

Piano Music for four hands: 10 variations on Schumann
theme (Op. 23), 16 waltzes (Op. 39); 33 Liebes-

lieder waltzes (Op. 52a and 65a), 21 Hungarian
Dances (without Op. number).

Two Pianos: Sonata (Op. 34a), Haydn variations
(Op. 56a).

Organ: 11 Chorale Preludes (Op. 122); Fugue in
A flat minor (without Op. number); Chorale
Prelude and fugue "O Traurigkeit" (without
Op. number); Fugues in A minor and G minor
(without Op. number).

Brahms himself made the following additional
arrangements of certain of the above works:—

Piano score with words.—Op. 12, 13, 17, 29, 42,
44, 45, 50, 53, 54, 55, 82, 109, 110.

Piano Solo.—Op. 39, Hungarian dances.

Piano duet.—Op. 11, 15, 16, 18, 25, 26, 36, 45,
51, 55, 67, 68, 73, 80, 81, 88, 90, 98, 111.

Two pianos, four hands.—Op. 15, 68, 73, 83, 90, 98.

Violin and piano.—Op. 120, Nos. 1 and 2.

Solo voice with piano.—Op. 103, Nos. 1-7, 11.

Orchestra.—Hungarian dances Nos. 1, 3, 10.

Practically all the chamber-music, except the
sonatas, can be had in excellent arrangements (not,
however, by Brahms) for two pianos, four hands, and
the symphonies, overtures and serenades for two
pianos, eight hands.

The clarinet quintet has been arranged as a
sonata for violin and piano; the two sextets for piano,
violin and cello, and the two string quartets, Op. 51,
for piano duet, violin and cello.

DISTINGUISHING MUSICAL CHARACTERISTICS

Throughout Brahms' music there occur certain characteristic methods of expression—his visiting cards—which, while not always unique with him, yet occur in his works so frequently and in such an individual way, as to make it possible for one familiar with his idiom to recognize it as his.

Perhaps the most prevalent in his use of cross-rhythms, much more startling in his day than to the modern world accustomed to jazz. Particularly characteristic are his cross-rhythms in slow time, three half-notes against four quarters, as in the first movement of the First Serenade, Op. 11, or four half-notes in 6/4 time, as in the 13th Psalm for Women's Chorus (Op. 27); or the more frequently occurring three-quarters against two, or against four eighths, as in the last movement of the Third Symphony, the first movement of the Fourth, the first movement of the F major quintet (Op. 88) (second theme), or of the A minor quartet (Op. 51, No. 2), and of the Clarinet Trio (22nd and 23rd bars). These slow triplet figures are uniquely Brahms. Practically every work contains a passage where he leaps suddenly out of the three rhythm into two; see, for example, the Scherzo of the Horn Trio, Op. 40, and in the third movement of the F Major Cello Sonata, Op. 99. Often he brings subtle rhythmic variation by introducing in triplet rhythm a figure which is essentially two-four or four-four, as in the piano passage just before the repeat in the last movement of the Horn Trio, in the

8th, 9th and 10th bars of the first movement of the
B flat quartet, or in the second bar of the C major
Intermezzo, Op. 119.   A most striking example of his
mixed rhythms is found in the beginning of the second
movement of the clarinet quintet (Op. 115) where the
five instruments play in five different rhythms at the
same time.

Many of Brahms' most characteristic melodies are
based on successive notes of a common chord.   Familiar
examples are the andante of the violin concerto, the
second theme (piano) of the Third Piano Quartet (C
minor, Op. 60), the Sapphishe Ode, the trios in the
Scherzos of the F minor piano quintet (Op. 34) and
the C major piano trio (Op. 87), and the opening theme
of the Clarinet Trio.   Frequently his melodies are
made by omitting one of the members of the triad,
usually the first or fifth, as in Feldeinsamkeit, Min-
nelied, the opening of the First Symphony, or the A
minor string quartet (Op. 51, No. 2), the second theme
of the E minor cello sonata (Op. 38), and the second
theme in the last movement of the A major Piano
Quartet (Op. 26).   This fondness for deleted arpeggios
is believed to be what really gives Kalbeck, Specht
and Niemann the material for their labored attempts
to find Brahms' motto F A F (frei aber froh) in his
works.   It is true that Joachim in his young days
adopted the motto F A E (frei aber einsam) which he
told Schumann signified "I am not engaged to be
married", and wrote a little piece based on these notes.
It may be that the unimportant opening piano accompaniment of the Second Ballade of Op. 10 announced
the motto (although F sharp, A, F sharp), but to

attempt to find it in the D minor concerto, or a combination of F A F and F A E in the opening of the
A minor quartet (dedicated not to Joachim but to
Billroth) or to blame on such a trivial idea the noble
opening of the Third Symphony (the A flat in the
middle is pronounced ASS in German) is believed to
be merely conjectural, and wholly inconsistent with
his reverence for his art, which, with him, was far
too holy to permit the indulgence in any personal whim.

Brahms had a special fondness for successive
thirds, sixths, and tenths, both for the piano, see the
opening piano passage in the early D minor concerto,
Op. 15, the andante of the Quintet, Op. 34, in the
second theme of the Second Symphony (letter K),
and for strings, see the second theme of the A major
Serenade, Op. 16, a very characteristic Brahms' passage, and the allegretto in the G minor piano quartet,
Op. 25. His interest in sixths and thirds and his
realization of the importance of their smooth execution
in playing his piano music, was perhaps what led him
to arrange the Chopin Etude in F minor as a study
in sixths and thirds.

Akin to the above is Brahms' habit of making a
melody or a connecting passage in descending intervals of a third, sometimes with another voice a tenth
below, of which the andante of the early F Minor
Piano Sonata is a typical example. Other instances
of this rather unique Brahms trait are the piano
passage just before the last return of the principal
theme in the first movement of the D Minor Violin
Sonata (Op. 108), the similar passage preceding the
return of the theme in the C Major Intermezzo (Op.

119), and the piano passage in the middle of the second of the Four Serious Songs (Op. 121).

A characteristic Brahms musical idiom is his dove-tailing of the voices to fill the bar. While this is a frequent melodic device with other composers, the different voices alternating with one another in stating the theme, with Brahms, (as sometimes with Beethoven) it is preeminently a rhythmic rather than a melodic feature. Illustrative are the two bars just before the entry of the second subject in the first movement of the clarinet quintet, the piano passage at the second statement of the principal theme in the C major trio (Op. 87), and the similar passage in G minor about half way through the first movement of the E flat clarinet sonata; see also the G minor Ballade for piano, Op. 118.

An example of the method by which Brahms added the rich romantic ornament to the classic structure and foundation, is in his treatment of sequences, not only in his descending suspended sevenths, as in the piano part in the trio of the Scherzo in the F minor Quintet, in the C major intermezzo for piano, Op. 119, the passage near the end of the sixth movement of the Requiem, and at the end of No. 4 (Fragen) of the Songs for Women's Chorus Op. 44 (which we can, of course, find in Bach and Veracini, though not so pungent); but more strikingly where, in the course of the sequence, he modulates momentarily from one key to that of the note next above, as in the theme of the Andante of the C Major Trio or in the 9th, 10th and 11th bars of the Andante of the Piano Quintet, or the rich D Major variation in the Andante of the Bb Major Sextet, or the passage near the end of the G Major String Quintet.

All great composers have, of course, understood the necessity and charm of contrast, but have achieved it in different ways. Brahms' use of contrast is nowhere better illustrated than in the passages by which, at the end of his development sections, he returns to the principal theme. Sometimes he does this by a bold modulation (as in the Andante of the Second Symphony) from a remote key (last movement of same), or by rhythmic uncertainty immediately succeeding a very marked rhythm (as in the Andante of the Fourth Symphony). Still more individual are the instances where he deliberately creates a seemingly unsolvable tangle, rhythmically, harmonically and melodically, which, as if by magic, suddenly smoothes itself into the serenity of the principal theme. An example of this deliberate spontaneity is the passage, already cited, at the end of the long pedal point on A in the first movement of the D minor violin sonata, and the descending fantasia-like duet between the clarinet and cello in the first movement of the Clarinet Quintet, immediately preceding the return to the simple principal theme in Brahms' favorite thirds.

Every now and then, Brahms indulges in a sort of orgy of throwing things in every direction,—a kind of musical pillow fight. There is a glorious page of this kind in the first movement of the Clarinet Quintet, another near the end of the first movement of the Fourth Symphony, and another in the last movement of the B major Trio (Op. 8).

A number of additional features have been emphasized in Brahms' music, such as his use of the harsh chord of the sixth instead of the tonic, his comparative avoidance of chromatic progressions, his use, particularly in his later works, of piano arpeggios of successive diminished sevenths. These can hardly, it is believed, be called individual Brahms, any more than can his superb use of pedal points, or his subtle accompaniments consisting of the theme in canon or in augmentation, diminution or inversion.

Additional examples of Brahms' "visiting cards" in the chamber music will be pointed out in the course of the following analysis of the different works.

THE PRINCIPAL BOOKS IN ENGLISH
ON BRAHMS

There are now in English a number of excellent biographies of Brahms, each of which contains a more or less elaborate analysis of his complete works, and all of which have been drawn on without compunction in the present essay. The monumental and meticulous treatise by Kalbeck has not yet been translated.

The sanest and most understanding book on Brahms is believed to be that by Fuller-Maitland, which, unfortunately, is out of print. Miss May gives more detail of his life and contains some charming personal recollections, she having been his piano pupil for several months in 1871 at Lichtenthal, near Baden-Baden. In the discussion of the music she occasionally gets over-sentimental but not so oppressively as Specht, who was intimate with Brahms in the later years and for that reason apparently believed that he could divine exactly what Brahms had in mind in composing each Opus, although he does not claim that Brahms ever confided this to him. Specht's description of Brahms' later environment and friends is most interesting and thoroughly worth while.

Niemann's book separates the life from the discussion of the works. The latter is convenient and the analyses are learned, but not very instructive except to an expert. Friedlander gives a history and analysis of each of the songs for one and two voices, like that here attempted for the chamber music. No singer of Brahms can afford to be without it.

Pulver is for the most part a mere succession of carefully verified dates, but is apparently devoid of any interest in or real understanding of the music. Of the Horn Trio, he says, "The Horn Trio is perhaps one of the finest compositions employing this intrument in a chamber work." Colles' is short and contains some very understanding thoughts on the music. Erb's little book is mainly quotations from the Reminiscences of Dietrich, Widmann, Henschel and Eugenie Schumann, all of which are now available in English. These Reminiscences, with the letters to and from the Schumanns (two volumes) (most of Brahms' to Frau Schumann he got back from her, with tears, in 1886, and threw them in the Rhine), the letters to and from Joachim and the Herzogenbergs (all translated) give a more correct and vivid idea of the man and his musical ideals than any biography. Daniel Gregory Mason's chapter on Brahms in his small volume "From Grieg to Brahms" is masterly in extracting the essence of what Brahms did for music. An interesting recent character study is that by Paul Krummeich, of the Music Faculty of the University of Pennsylvania, in the April, 1932, number of the General Magazine of the University. Mr. Krummeich writes authoritatively not only as a profound student of Brahms, but as a finished performer of his music, both for piano, violin and viola.

NOTES ON THE CHAMBER MUSIC
(In the order of their proposed performance in the Philadelphia Centenary Series)

TRIO IN A MINOR, FOR PIANO, CLARINET AND CELLO, OP. 114

In 1881, Brahms had been introduced by Bülow (conductor at Meiningen, and after the first Symphony one of Brahms' staunchest supporters) to the music-loving Duke Georg and his consort, Baroness von Heldburg, after which he was often a welcome and happy visitor at the palace, where a regal suite was always at his disposal and he was allowed for the most part to do about as he pleased, in return for which he cheerfully donned for dinner the much despised full-dress suit.

Preceding the season of 1890–91 he went through a period of depression and discouragement. To a friend he wrote "I have tormented myself to no purpose lately and till now I never had to do so at all; things always came easily to me." In March, 1891, he paid a visit to Meiningen, the Duke having invited as one of the party, at Brahms' request, his friend Widmann, who, in his Reminiscences, gives a charming account of Brahms' genial and happy status, not only with the fine musicians of the Court Orchestra, but also with the "exalted personages" of the Court set, before whom Brahms never felt or showed the slightest embarrassment. During this visit Brahms became intensely interested in the clarinet, through hearing the Court clarinetist, Richard Mühlfeld (originally a violinist, who had taught himself the clarinet). On March 17th he wrote to Frau Schumann

[45]

at Frankfort telling her of a performance of "the very fine F minor Concerto (by Weber) for the Clarinet". "It is impossible," he says, "to play the clarinet better than Herr Mühlfeld does here." "He is absolutely the best I know". (Brahms used whimsically to introduce him as "Fraulein von Mühlfeld, meine prima donna")

At Brahms' request, Mühlfeld gave him a private recital, playing him one piece after another and discussing his instrument. There resulted, during the next May and June at Ischl, the Clarinet Trio and Quintet.

These two works were first performed from manuscript at a private concert at Meiningen on November 24, 1891, and in public in Berlin on December 12, where they were received (especially the quintet) with tremendous enthusiasm. At this concert, Joachim broke his rule of thirty years standing to permit no instruments other than strings at his quartet performances in Berlin. On November 25th, Brahms, from Meiningen, wrote Simrock of the plans for the Berlin concert, where he proposed, with "Klavier und Klarinette," to invade "das keusche Heiligtum," whereby "das Joachimsche Streichquartett leider durch mich seine Jungfernschaft verliert". Later in the winter Mühlfeld came to London for performances of the two works, which were given there with great success in March. In 1895 Miss May heard Mühlfeld and Hausmann play this Trio, with Brahms at the piano, and Joachim turning the pages.

In an interesting magazine article published in 1897, Ferdinand Schumann, Clara's grandson, tells us that Brahms considered the timbre of the clarinet better suited to that of the piano than that of stringed instruments.

This Trio is little known and its beauties are, it is believed, much underestimated. Miss May calls it "one of the least convincing of his works". Colles says that it sounds like a study for the instrument. Fuller-Maitland (the most ardent Brahman of them all) characterizes the theme of the Andantino (with the opening theme of the E flat clarinet sonata) as the only two really "commonplace" melodies in Brahms. Niemann, although praising the slow movement, says that the Trio is outshone by the radiance of the Quintet.

Specht alone has a good word for it, but considers that "it sings of love alone."

Although as a whole doubtless ranking below the Quintet, it is by no means "inferior." The Adagio is one of Brahms' most deeply beautiful movements, the opening reminding one of that in the slow movement of the D minor violin sonata. The eighth bar, where the cello comes up to take the theme, is one of the lovely spots one never tires of hearing. Later, in the piano part, there comes a striking example of Brahms' rich modulated sequence. The Andantino (like the Allegretto in the F Minor Clarinet Sonata) must not be taken so seriously. It does not "sing of love" or of anything else important. It is merely a nice tune, in a sort of Greater Tschaikowsky vein, giving the clarinet a chance to show off all his pretty tricks, which Brahms develops in so interesting a way as to make it fresh each time it is played, and to which he appends a little extra eleven bar coda which is a veritable gem, even for Brahms, each note an essential part in the musical scheme. Except for the Adagio, the Trio is not nearly as beautiful with the viola substituted for the clarinet.

The last movement is full of startling and most interesting rhythmic changes and contains one of his characteristic themes descending in intervals of a third, here for sixteen successive notes.

Let the critics first study this Trio until they are sure they understand it all, by which time they may share Joachim's revised estimate. In preparation for the first London performance he played the clarinet part on the viola, before Mühlfeld's arrival, so as to accustom Miss Davies and Piatti to the work, after which he wrote Brahms: "I like the piece better and better."

SONATA IN G MAJOR FOR PIANO AND VIOLIN, OP. 78

This Sonata, while perhaps not as "popular" as the A major, or as great as the D minor, is probably the most beloved of the three; certainly it was by Brahms' three musical intimates, Joachim, Clara Schumann and Elizabet von Herzogenberg. It is typical of his serene maturity, in the quiet summer mood of the clarinet quintet, with none of the "storm and stress" and bottled-up energy characteristic of such works as the D minor concerto or the piano quintet.

Although the first violin sonata which Brahms published, it was the fourth which he completed. The first (in A minor) was finished before October, 1853, when he wrote Joachim that "Dr. Schumann suggests" that he publish it as Op. 5. This A minor sonata was apparently lent to Liszt to play with Remenyi after the visit at Weimar in August, 1853, and lost between them. In 1872, Wasielewski showed Brahms' intimate friend Deitrich the violin part of a violin sonata, which the latter immediately recognized as in Brahms' handwriting and believed to belong to this lost sonata. We may hope that the whole will still be found. Two other violin sonatas were destroyed by him as unsatisfactory.

After the G major sonata was introduced to the public in early 1880 (on a concert tour by Brahms and Joachim through the Austrian provinces), Joachim played it wherever he went, with the result that it brought Brahms more new friends than perhaps any of his other works. Its effect on both Clara Schumann and Elizabet von Herzogenberg was to rouse deep emotion. Elizabet's husband quotes the opening phrase in his first letter to Brahms after her death. Billroth wrote that "if it were played as we hear it with our inner ear, we should be unable to restrain our tears." After receiving the manuscript, Clara Schumann wrote to Brahms:

> "I must send a line to tell you how deeply excited I am over your sonata. It came today; of course I at once played it through, and at the end could not help bursting into tears of joy over it. After the first delicate charming movement and the second, you can imagine my rapture, when in the third I once more found my passionately loved melody with the delightful quaver rhythm."

Frau Schumann here refers to the fact that both the principal theme of the last movement and its piano obligato are taken bodily from the songs Regenlied and Nachtklang, Op. 59, Nos. 3 and 4.

On June 16, 1890, then in her seventy-second year, she sent a postcard to Brahms at Ischl:

> "Joachim was here on the 8th (Roberts' eightieth birthday) and for two days we had a lot of music. We played the Regenlieder Sonata again and I revelled in it once more. I always wish that the last movement might accompany me in my journey from here to the next world. Farewell, I hope you are well and happy. Ever yours, Cl. Sch."

The opening of the first movement, (after the 8th bar) contains typical illustrations, both of Brahms' cross-rhythms and of his use of arpeggios in the piano part, not as a mere brilliant accompaniment, but as an essential and integral part of the musical conception.

This sonata is one of several chamber works in which Brahms introduces the principal theme of the first movement in the coda of the last (see also the B flat string quartet, Op. 67, and the clarinet quintet, Op. 115). Here, indeed, the principal theme of the finale is a transformation of that with which the sonata begins. The final coda, which is one of the most precious bits of Brahms, summarizes the whole work with unbelievable simplicity,—simplicity by elimination in its most perfect form.

SEXTET IN B FLAT MAJOR FOR STRINGS, OP. 18

This comparatively early work (1860) is one of the few major compositions by Brahms which was universally liked at first hearing. It dates from his stay in Hamburg (after the completion of his three seasons in Detmold), one of the happiest periods of his life, the period of the Ladies' Choir in which he so delighted.

Specht ascribes the choice of the key B flat (which is B in German, B natural being called H) to his then enthusiasm, Bertha Porubszky (she afterward married Arthur Faber and they became two of his most faithful friends; it was for her, at the birth of her first child, that he wrote the Wiegenlied). It is fortunate that in German "Clara" is spelled with a K, whereby Specht is deprived of the chance to make Frau Schumann responsible for all Brahms' gloomy C minor moods. She first refers to the B flat Sextet in a letter to Joachim on October 11, 1860, nine days before its initial performance by Joachim and his colleagues at Hanover. On November 27th they played it at the Conservatoire at Leipsic, where Frau Schumann had gone to hear his A major Serenade. She records that it was "exquisitely played and roused decided enthusiasm."

This Sextet, more than any other work, endeared Brahms to the Viennese. He took it there (with the two piano quartets, Op. 25 and 26) on his first visit in September, 1862, and at its first performance by the Hellmesberger party, all the skeptical critics were converted.

Neimann's musical analysis of this Sextet (pp. 295-298) is particularly interesting, pointing out the homophonic structure as compared with the later and more romantic Sextet in G major, and also tracing the classic influence of the Schubert Forellen Quintet and of the Beethoven Septet and Pastoral Symphony.

The opening theme is one of the lovely diatonic melodies, simple as a folk-song, which makes one wonder how Brahms can be thought unmelodious. Originally the movement began at the present bar eleven, but Joachim suggested the little ten bar fore-word by the two cellos and viola. It is interesting to know that Brahms welcomed from Joachim and often adopted suggestions of substance like this, while he sometimes refused to listen to criticisms relative to the technique of the violin,—ways to make the string music more playable—from this supreme master of the instrument. Particularly striking is the sudden modulation to the second subject, pianissimo, in A major. The movement depends for its charm largely on the tossing about of the different ideas between the six instruments and is less interesting in the arrangement for two pianos than other works which are less successful in the original form.

The Andante and Variations was originally for piano solo and so performed frequently by Clara Schumann. Brahms himself played it for Miss May in 1871. His version in this form has never, however, been published. Especially beautiful is the variation in D major with its characteristic rich modulation F major, G minor, E minor, D minor. There is also an amusing little music box variation following it.

Of the Scherzo, Clara Schumann writes, after a most enthusiastic performance by Joachim in London, "Was it your idea that it should be played extremely fast? I like it fast but severe." The Trio of the Scherzo is one of the places referred to in the general description of Brahms' music, where he throw things in every direction, uncontrolled and uproarious.

In the last movement Brahms turns his sextet of instruments into two string trios, treated antiphonally. This movement, with its beautiful long round themes, each growing out of that which precedes it, never fails to please, and the spirited ending always provokes a storm of applause.

TRIO IN B MAJOR FOR PIANO, VIOLIN & CELLO, OP. 8

Through this Trio we see Brahms for the one and only time actually at work. He wrote it during the winter of 1853–4, before he was twenty-one, and rewrote it in the summer of 1889 when he was past sixty-six. Both versions are published, though the early one (Augener) is harder to get. Their comparison gives us the best possible insight into what Brahms believed he had learned during the intervening forty-five years. (The revision of the A major Serenade is not so instructive).

In the middle of March, 1854, Dietrich wrote to Naumann from Düsseldorf to tell of Schumann's attempted suicide three weeks before, adding "Brahms has written a wonderful new trio." In Clara's diary we find the following vivid passages:

"Sunday 26th (March, 1854). In the evening Brahms played me his wonderful new trio, at Frl. Leser's, but I do not entirely understand it. I cannot quite get used to the constant change of tempo in his works, and besides he plays them so entirely according to his own fancy that today, for example, though I was reading the music, I could not follow him, and it was very difficult for his fellow players to keep their places. But there are some splendid things in this piece. Brahms was not very polite; it seems to me that he will be spoiled by the tremendous idolatry with which he is treated by the younger generation, for he often expresses himself in a way which I never heard my Robert, for instance. I am afraid that he will often 'put his foot in it' as they say. I am very sorry for this, but I should not have the courage to tell him of it."

"April 17th * * * Joachim and Hermann

Grimm [son of one of the fairy-tale brothers] paid me an unexpected visit this morning * * * We at once played the Brahms trio, which Joachim did not know yet. How he played it at sight, without one mistake! Now, for the first time, one really heard the trio properly. * * * In the evening we repeated the trio, and now everything in it is clear to me."

"November 21st. Later Brahms played his trio (B major). It leaves nothing to be wished except another first movement; I cannot get to like this one, though I think the opening magnificent. The second, third, and fourth movements are quite worthy of his genius."

The first public performance of this trio was in New York, by William Mason, Theodore Thomas and Carl Bergmann, on November 27, 1855.

Hanslick, the distinguished Viennese critic and ardent Brahms enthusiast, censured this first version as "immature workmanship." Apparently there smouldered in Brahms' soul both a secret love of this work and a consciousness that it was not what it should be. On September 3, 1889, he writes from Ischl to Frau Schumann at Baden:

"With what childish amusement I whiled away the beautiful summer days you will never guess. I have rewritten my B major trio and can call it Op. 108 instead of Op. 8. It will not be so wild as it was before, but whether it will be better——?"

On September 20th he came to Baden.

"September 21st. Brahms played me the B major trio which he has been rewriting * * * The Trio seems to me much improved."

In November she wrote suggesting that he play the Trio at the coming Museum concert, and he answered:

"How gladly would I play my trio there, for it would be a sign that it still pleased me a little. Unfortunately, however, it does not please me at all,—not in the least, and as I have not this pleasure I must renounce the other one."

Three months later, however, we have another letter showing what a child he really was:—

"Vienna, February 23rd.

DEAR CLARA:

From the enclosed letter from Hanslick, which I should be obliged if you would kindly return to me some time, you will see that yesterday there was a rehearsal and performance of my B major trio. I had already thrown the piece to the dogs and did not want to play it. The fact that it seemed inadequate to me and did not please me means little. When it came to be discussed, however, no curiosity was expressed, but everybody, even Joachim and Wüllner, for instance, started off by saying how much pleasure they had in playing the old piece quite recently, and had found it full of sentiment and romantic and heaven knows what else.

And now I am glad that I did play it after all. It was a very jolly day, for Billroth, too, was able to be there in the evening.

I only feel sorry that I have not played it to you also, that is to say that I did not accept the Chamber Music Evening. I suppose it is too late now? Otherwise I should feel tempted * * * *"

After receiving the new version, Elizabet von Herzogenberg writes:

"I feel that you had no right to intrude your master touch on this lovable, if sometimes vague, production of your youth."

In March, Frau Schumann wrote a friend:

"We expect Brahms on the 21st of this month when he is to play his newly rewritten Trio in B major at a quartet evening. It has been a great success in Buda-Pest and Vienna. Most of the motifs remain, but the way in which they are worked out is quite different."

From the Diary:

"Monday, March 17th. Brahms arrived * * * He seems in very good spirits and there is every reason why he should be."

"18th. He rehearsed his rewritten Trio, Op. 8, with Heermann and Becker. I felt rather desperate, his playing was so wanting in clearness, and there were also many things that I could not follow."

"19th. He rehearsed again at the Sommerhoffs and today I understood it better. I was particularly pleased with the first movement, but it does not carry me away as the C minor Trio does."

"March 22nd. Quartet evening at the Museum. A Brahms evening * * * the audience was very animated; in the Trio, the scherzo roused most enthusiasm * * * The whole Trio strikes me as much better proportioned than it was but I do not altogether like it. * * * the second subject of the last movement seems to me quite horrible. The first subject of the same movement is heavenly, and then the second with iron hand suddenly hurls one down from the skies."

The principal changes are for compactness. The original first movement, especially, was long-drawn out, with two elaborate fugal development sections. In the revised version the three original themes are condensed to two, the only one of the three retained being the first, one of the most lovable of Brahms' diatonic tunes. The second theme in this revised movement (G sharp minor, beginning with three descending steps of a third) is one of the weird haunting kind that characterizes his later period. If you like it, you like Brahms, if you do not, you may some day. It is superbly developed to a grand climax after which he slides back into the recapitulation of the principal theme imperceptibly and unexpectedly, with the uncanny skill of Brahms' full maturity. There follows a lovely new coda with triplet figures in the piano ending with Brahms' favorite plagal cadence.

The Scherzo is scarcely altered in the new version, except for a new coda which disintegrates into its atoms and evaporates into nothingness,—different from anything else in Brahms, but clearly Brahms nevertheless. The Trio of the Scherzo is a Brahms tune which one cannot hear too often,—as inevitable as folk-music. The Adagio is greatly condensed, the second theme (a deliberate quotation, says Kalbeck, from Schubert's Am Meer) omitted, as well as the middle section, and a new melodious cello theme, with queer halting piano passages, inserted new. The

weird passage of high triplets on the piano is *not* late
Brahms but taken bodily from the original version of
1854. The movement most drastically dealt with is
the finale in B minor, from which Brahms has eliminated the beautiful singing cello theme of the original
and substituted, with much condensation, the robust
bumptious second subject to which Frau Schumann
so strongly objected. The working out of this movement, with its hammering principal theme, is superb
and it reaches an utterly satisfying conclusion, the
struggle triumphant, like the end of the D minor
violin sonata.

SONATA IN F MINOR FOR CLARINET AND PIANO OPUS 120, No. 1

During the summer of 1894, Brahms returned to the Clarinet (the Trio and Quintet dating from his introduction to the instrument by Mühlfeld in 1891), and composed the two sonatas comprising Opus 120, which were said to have been written for "Piano and Mühlfeld" rather than for "Piano and Clarinet". In November he came to Frankfurt with Mühlfeld on purpose to play them to Frau Schumann and Joachim. She tells in her diary of her delight in hearing both of them four times during this visit.

Specht thinks "he is not wrong in assuming" that both clarinet sonatas are obituary love poems to Elizabet von Herzogenberg, (who had died two years before), but does not say that Brahms told him this, in which case he would have been sure of it. What there is in either sonata to suggest one calling "woefully and bitterly into the void" it is difficult to imagine.

The first sonata in F minor, begins in the serious mood of the Piano Quintet, with a noble theme, the big sweeping skips of which are peculiarly suitable to the clarinet. Particularly noticeable in the first movement is the rhythmic tangle about three-quarters way through, where against the clarinet's three quarter-notes the piano has four dotted eighths, with four arpeggio sixteenths to each clarinet note and three to each in the piano melody. This combination of the rhythmic 3/4, 4/4 and 9/12, produces a unique effect, causing an involuntary catching of the breath, followed by a sigh of relief as it untangles itself on the last beat of the third bar. At the close of this movement is one of Brahms' incomparable codas, perfectly adapted to the clarinet.

The Andante in A flat Major is wholly different from anything else in Brahms. It is essentially for the clarinet, and loses most of its individuality when played on the viola. It is futile to attempt to describe it.

The wonder of the Allegretto is that at sixty-one Brahms could write as freshly and joyously as at twenty. Like the Andantino of the clarinet Trio it is not intended to be serious or important, but light and amusing. Note the canon between the clarinet and the left hand of the piano after the first repeat, followed by two piano bars of 2/4 rhythm in 3/4 time, also Brahms' favorite thirds in the Trio section.

The last movement, vivace, is a rondo, built around three Fs in half-notes on the piano, followed by a rollicking tune, mingled with typical Brahms' slow triplets. The middle section furnishes another example of simplicity by elimination, so much said with so few notes. Toward the end are passages strongly reminiscent of the opening of the D minor violin sonata, and of the last movements of the C minor piano quartet and the A major violin sonata. The movement ends brilliantly and conclusively. Brahms knew always when and how to stop.

SEXTET IN G MAJOR, FOR STRINGS, OP. 36

While the First Sextet (Op. 18, B flat major) may always be the most popular, being the easiest to grasp quickly, the Second is generally conceded to be the greater of the two; its possibilities for new pleasure at each new hearing or performance are unending.

At least one movement of this Sextet (the Adagio) was originally in the form of a string quartet, composed early in 1855, almost ten years before the Sextet was completed. On February 7, 1855, Brahms, from Düsseldorf, wrote to Frau Schumann (on a concert tour in Holland):— "This evening I wished to copy the whole of the Adagio from the Quartet, but I cannot finish it. I must stop in order to write you a few words". Then follows four bars of music, on one staff, constituting (but for a few unimportant notes) the first violin and first viola parts of what subsequently became the opening of the Adagio of the Sextet.

Frau Schumann got back from Rotterdam on February 10th and Brahms must have played her the new quartet. Almost ten years later, on New Year's day 1865, she writes to him acknowledging with delight her receipt from him, two days before, of a manuscript which, from her comments, was evidently the G Major Sextet.

"To think", she says, "of a big work like that and that I had no suspicion of it" . . . . . "The theme [quoting the murmuring viola quaver figure on G and F sharp which continues through the first movement] might easily be stolen from you, but what could anyone else do with it, who did not understand, as you do, how to surround it with charming and expressive *motifs* con-

stantly interplaying and forming themselves into
a chain of delightful thoughts. I particularly
like the tone of this movement, it is so soft and
delicate. The development has once more delighted me—one can always look forward to this
with special pleasure in your work. It is not
with you, as it is with others, a medley of skillful
combinations by which emotion is driven more
or less into the background; with you it seems
as if only then did all the *motifs* find their warmest
and truest expression, and that is what is so
delightful. I also like the Scherzo very much,
it is fresh and interesting from beginning to end.
The first theme in the Adagio at once struck me as
familiar in times gone by—in which of your pieces
had you it before? . . . . "

Joachim next had the manuscript and wrote Frau
Schumann an interesting letter about it on February
3rd. "The Adagio", he says, "looks heavenly and
typical of Brahms"—

On July 26, 1865, she writes from Baden to Hermann Levi:

"Johannes came with his Sextet which he has
arranged for four hands—It is quite charming;
full of spirit and delicacy". (This does not refer
to the First Sextet, of which she had received the
four-hand arrangement from Brahms May 29,
1861, having played it with him three weeks
before.)

Although privately given both for strings and in
the four-hand version (Billroth writes in April, 1866,
that we "purged" ourselves with it after hearing
Liszt's Symphonic poems on two pianos), this Sextet
was not publicly performed until early in 1867, when
Hellmesberger gave it in Vienna. It was wholly unap-

preciated. It is amusing to compare the following contemporary criticisms with that of Beethoven's three Sonatas (quoted *supra* p. 23) and again with Frau Schumann's understanding comment just given:—

> "Brahms may be called a virtuoso in the modern development of the quartet style . . . . . but only that can reach the heart which proceeds from the heart, and the Sextet comes from the hand and the head, whilst the warm pulsations of the heart are to be felt only at intervals."

* * * * *

> "We are always seized with a kind of oppression when the new John in the wilderness, Herr Johannes Brahms, announces himself. This prophet, proclaimed by Robert Schumann in his darkening hours . . . . . makes us quite disconsolate with his impalpable, dizzy tone-vexations that have neither body nor soul and can only be products of the most desperate effort. Such manifest glaring, artificiality is quite peculiar to this gentleman. How many drops of perspiration may adhere to these note-heads?"

As a result of a letter to Härtels by a "donkey" (Clara Schumann to Brahms, December 22, 1866) who said that the Sextet was "too mad" for him, Härtels, the publishers, returned it and Brahms sent it to Simrock.

> "They [Härtels] must" Clara continues, "already be savage about it and he must be feeling ashamed . . . . . I feel less angry over the stupidity of such people than over their infamy in thus passing sentence of death upon a work on which a composer has spent all the strength of his soul. But fortunately, it has not succeeded and the tide is now turning."

Joachim persisted with the Sextet and finally the public began, as Frau Schumann had predicted, to understand it. Fuller-Maitland instances the performance of this Sextet by Joachim and his fellows as the perfection of chamber music, suggesting "perennial youth".

In the letters of Theodor Billroth, the distinguished Viennese surgeon and Brahms' intimate friend, there is an amusing allusion to this Sextet which strikes a sympathetic note for all amateur performers of Brahms' chamber music. Brahms had been asked to a music party at Billroth's house in the summer of 1866 to hear a performance of the new Sextet. Billroth, who was a fine musician, both pianist and violinist, was to take the second viola part, but at the last moment the presence of the composer so unnerved him that he surrendered his viola to his teacher, Eschmann, who was in the invited party, to Brahms' great amusement.

This Sextet has come in for its full share of sentimental analysis by reason of the fact that it was composed shortly after Brahms abandoned the idea of marrying Agathe von Siebold, the attractive daughter of a professor at Göttingen. Brahms himself admitted that the recurring phrase in the second theme group, A G A H E, was intentionally a farewell to her, but to say that, because of this little phrase the whole is a "sadly sweet remembrance grown into serenity" or to contend that the E flat—B flat in the third and fourth bars of the main theme represent "intertwining" Es (or S) for Siebold, and B for Brahms, is wholly fanciful. The only movement which might reasonably be imagined as "sadly reminiscent" would

be the Adagio, which as we have seen, Brahms had composed ten years before in the form of a string quartet.

The truth about Agathe seems to be that while,
for a time, she was an attractive possibility, after the
very hostile reception of the D minor concerto in
Leipsic, Brahms decided that he was too much a failure
to consider marriage (see the Widmann Reminiscences).

In a letter from Frau Schumann to Brahms dated
February 5, 1860, she reveals the situation:—

> "I was very miserable in Cassel. I could not
> get poor Agathe, and many other things, out of
> my head. I kept on seeing the poor lonely girl,
> and I felt all her grief. Ah! dear Johannes, if
> only you had not allowed it to go so far!"

The first movement is in the "morning joy"
mood of the G major violin sonata and the clarinet
quintet, and is one of the most wonderful movements
in chamber music, with the subtlest touches throughout. Much of the perfect mastery of form in this
movement (as well as the depth in the Andante) we
would have expected to find only in a later work.
The second theme in D major is one of the most woe-
dispelling in Brahms, and the trio of the delicate
Scherzo is one of the most carefree of his tunes, a
rollicking waltz. The Andante Hanslick wittily and
inappropriately called "Variations on no theme". The
last movement (not in notes merely, but in the whole
idea and in all the themes) is remarkably like
Tschaikowski's Serenade for Strings, Op. 48, written
in 1880, fourteen years after the publication of this
Sextet. This is interesting in view of Tschaikowski's
aversion to Brahms' music, which he considered the
work of a mere learned pedant.

QUARTET IN C MINOR, FOR STRINGS, OP. 51 No. 1

The two quartets, in C Minor and A Minor, Op. 51, were published, as Brahms told a friend, Alwin Cranz, only after he had written and discarded twenty others.

In Brahms' letter to Joachim in October 1853, relative to the works which Schumann recommends him to publish, he specifies a Quartet in B flat (the unerring Dr. Altmann says that Schumann wanted him to publish as Op. 1 a quartet in B minor). We have already noted the Adagio in E Minor from the quartet written in 1855, and subsequently turned into the G Major Sextet.

In Frau Schumann's diary for October, 1856, she speaks of Johannes having "composed a wonderfully beautiful Adagio for his C sharp minor quartet—full of tenderness." This, however, may have been what subsequently became the C Minor Piano Quartet (see infra p. 116). In the dairy in August, 1866, she records Johannes having arrived with a full beard (at which she is most indignant, "it quite spoils the refinement of his face") and having "played me some magnificent numbers from a German Requiem and also a string quartet in C Minor. I am most moved by the Requiem. . . ."

The two quartets were not finished and given to the world until 1873. They are dedicated to Theodore Billroth, Brahms' surgeon-viola friend in Vienna. That in C minor is one of his most pitiless though one of his most profound works. Except for the slow movement, so resembling that in the piano quintet, there is no compromising. If Brahms were all like this he

might be termed harsh and his disciples be invited to
enjoy him as our grandparents used to give us various
bitter medicines, unpleasant to take, but good for us
after absorbing. As a matter of fact, Brahms is not at
all like that. One needs no Sunday clothes or hair shirt
to enjoy him. His music is full to overflowing with
humanity. It is only occasionally that he seems to
crush down all tenderness.

Niemann contends that the key of C Minor means
to Brahms "hard, pitiless struggle and defiance", but
fails to reconcile the last movement of the C minor
piano quartet, the allegretto of the G minor piano
quartet, and that of the Third Symphony.

SONATA IN A MAJOR, FOR VIOLIN AND PIANO, OP. 100

This Sonata is commonly known as the Thun Sonata, because written at Thun where Brahms spent the three summers 1886–7–8, near his friend Widmann. It is also sometimes called the Meistersinger Sonata, because of the similarity, (seized and insisted on by the anti-Brahms crowd with wholly unnecessary acrimony), of the first three notes to the first three in Walters' Prize Song. The latter resemblance is merely superficial, and certainly accidental. The similarity is no more striking than the resemblance of the next phrase of the Prize Song to bars 21 and 22 of the C sharp minor fugue in the second book of the Well-Tempered Clavichord, which apparently has never been held against Wagner. Brahms used to be extremely irritated whenever some pedant remarked on these chance similarities. "Any ass could see that" he once said to one who "regretted" that the C major theme at the end of his First Symphony was like the Freude theme in Beethoven's Ninth. "What matters is not the sequence of notes in a theme, but only the way in which a musician makes it his own fruitful possession."

This Sonata, with the F major Cello Sonata (Op. 99) and the C minor trio (Op. 101), was written in the summer of 1886, and had its first performance at Widmann's house at Berne, near Thun, where Brahms used to spend practically all his week-ends during these summer sojourns, walking over with a knapsack of books which he had borrowed on the previous Monday, enveloped, on rainy days, in a huge shawl, fastened in front by a large pin. Widmann wrote a

fairy ballad about the Sonata which Miss May trans-
lates in full (Vol. II p. 224) and with which Brahms
was much pleased, often later writing to Widmann for
additional copies.

From Frau Schumann's diary of June, 1887, a
period of suffering for her both from physical ailments
and from anxiety for her son Ferdinand:—

> "God be thanked there was some music
> again on the 18th, at the Heermann's [leader of
> the Heerman quartet at Frankfurt]. I played
> Johannes' A Major Sonata with him for the first
> time. It was a pleasure which made me forget
> all my misery for one evening. This Sonata is a
> beautiful, noble work. I like the first and last
> movements best, the theme of the last is drawn
> out in the most heavenly way. The Adagio does
> not seem to me to have enough genuine feeling,
> it is more reflective". (How could she say this
> about the last section, just before the coda?)

The Thun Sonata is the best-known of the three,
and the easiest to grasp at first hearing. The first
movement is in a thoroughly comfortable and contented mood. It typifies the skill with which Brahms
welded his violin and piano parts together. The
second theme gives an echo of the song Wie Melodien
Op. 105, No. 1, and the last of Auf dem Kirchhofe
No. 4 from the same Opus (composed before the
Sonata).

The second movement combines the usual slow
movement and scherzo by alternating with the quiet
meditative mood of the opening theme in F major, the
sprightly vivace in D minor, with its dainty dialogue.

The little coda is utterly satisfactory. Heinrich von Herzogenberg, Elizabet's worthy and pedantic husband, had the temerity to suggest to Brahms that the vivace theme was reminiscent of Grieg's G Minor Violin Sonata.

The last movement gives us the most ecstatic tune in Brahms' chamber music, a broad, luscious theme of easy spaciousness and saturated intensity. Its full freshness does not survive repeated hearing, however, as does that of the Andante of the D minor. This last movement was originally longer, the coda having been materially cut down by Brahms, (so he told Joachim who told Miss May) leaving for us another of his matchless summaries. What treasures are the last ten bars of each of the ten movements of the three violin sonatas!

QUARTET IN G MINOR FOR PIANO, VIOLIN, VIOLA AND CELLO, OP. 25

The two piano quartets Op. 25 and 26 in G minor and A major were composed, according to Niemann, as early as 1856, but like the other works of the period, were held back and polished and repolished, and published only in 1863, after repeated public performances. When tried over with Bargheer and two others of the Detmold orchestra they found the original string parts of the G minor quartet ungrateful and sometimes unplayable, resulting in considerable alteration.

It was with this quartet that Brahms made his bow to Vienna. Shortly after his arrival in September, 1862, he went to call on the kindly, generous and ever youthful Julius Epstein. "My name is Johannes Brahms", he said as he entered. Epstein, who was well acquainted with his already published works, hearing that he had with him two new piano quartets, at once summoned Joseph Hellmesberger, the leading quartet player in Vienna, to a rehearsal, followed by breakfast, (in the house where Mozart wrote Figaro). At the conclusion of the G minor, Hellmesberger startled young Brahms by falling on his neck, exclaiming "This is Beethoven's heir", and announcing that they must play the quartet at their next concert, which they did on October 14th, arousing great interest, considerable praise, some scorn, much discussion pro and con,—an auspicious beginning for Brahms' Vienna career.

From that time on, the G minor quartet has been a prime favorite with the public, being much the most frequently heard of the three. With the B flat Sextet,

and the A major violin Sonata, it is the easiest of
Brahms' chamber works—to use Brahms' own phrase—
to "hear at sight".

Clara Schumann did not wholly approve of it.
She wrote him a rather extended criticism in July,
1861:—

> "There is much in the movement of the G
> minor quartet that I like—and much that I care
> for less. The first part seems to me too little
> G minor and too much D major, and I think
> that owing to lack of the former, it loses
> clarity . . . .
> "It is so beautiful where the piano joins in
> triplets . . . . I cannot help thinking that if
> you had me in mind at all when you were writing
> it, you must have known that I should be charmed
> with the scherzo in C minor. In fact, I should
> hardly call it a scherzo at all. I can only think
> of it as an allegretto. But it is a piece after my
> own heart . . . . . . You are certainly smil-
> ing at me and thinking that I am not aware of
> the higher value of the first movement. Cer-
> tainly I am; but in the C minor part I find
> myself so tenderly transported to dreamland that
> it is as if my soul was rocked to sleep by the
> notes." . . . .

From the diary:—

> "Nov. 14, (1862)
> "A rehearsal of Johannes' G minor quartet"—
> "Nov. 16th—
> "A soireè of mine—I was frightfully nervous.
> It may have been anxiety about the quartet,
> which I had so much at heart. The fiddlers
> scratched away or slept, although I put my
> whole heart into it. The last movement took the

audience by storm. The quartet only partially satisfies me, there is too little unity in the first movement, and the emotion in the Adagio is too forced, without really carrying me away. But I love the Allegretto in C minor and the last movement."

This quartet is essentially fresh and vigorous, full of vitality. Niemann's musical analysis points out most interestingly in what Brahms departs from the methods of the classic masters (see his p. 279). Of especial interest, in the first movement, is the introduction of the second theme in D minor prior to its subsequent full statement in D major, giving an impression of lavish richness; also the evaporation to nothingness after the climax. The Andante recalls a super-Mendelssohn. The middle section, in C major, is reminiscent of the spirit of the trio of the scherzo in the B major Piano Trio. The Intermezzo abounds in Brahms' favorite sixths, thirds and tenths.

The last movement is the famous "Rondo alla Zingarese", riotously brilliant, with its astonishing imitation of the dulcimer; perfectly direct, with no puzzling entanglements, wayward rhythms or baffling syncopations. In 1858 Joachim had made a great success with his Hungarian Concerto. Generous soul that he was, he told Brahms that with this Rondo Brahms had "beaten him on his own ground". Dating from his tour with Remenyi, Brahms had a special passion for the gypsy music and used to sit for hours while the gypsy bands delighted to play to him. The first of the Hungarian dances were written before October, 1858. Illustrative of his fondness for Hungarian folk music and its influence in his works are, besides the Gypsy Songs (Op 103 and the last four of Op. 112), the piano variations on a Hungarian theme, Op. 21, No. 2, the last movement of the A major quartet Op. 26, several numbers in the Waltzes for four hands, Op. 39, the B minor Capriccio in Op. 76, the Andante of the C major Trio, Op. 87, the last movement of the B flat piano Concerto, Op. 83, the finale of the G major string quintet, and the middle section of the Adagio of the clarinet quintet.

TRIO IN C MAJOR, FOR PIANO, VIOLIN AND CELLO OP. 87

It is difficult to understand why the C Major Trio is so little known and so seldom played It fully merits a better acquaintance. Of the three, it seems the brightest and most joyous, and contains little of the "heaven storming Johannes". The gloomy Specht, however, calls it a "personal confession" (of what?). Niemann, a most learned and thorough musician, prefers it to the C minor.

When Clara Schumann received the manuscript in August, 1882, she was "delighted with it."

"A trio like yours was a real musical tonic . . . . . How I would love to hear it properly played—All I have is a poor little upright piano. I love every movement and how wonderfully it is developed. I am so charmed with the way in which one motif grows out of another, and phrase follows phrase. The scherzo is exquisite, as is also the andante with its lively theme which must sound quite original in the placing of the double octaves. How fresh the last movement is, and, moreover, interesting in its thoroughly artistic combinations."

She then begs permission to mention a "few small points", one of which Brahms apparently adopted, but another (the elimination of the two turns by the violin in the coda of the first movement) he ignored. Strangely enough, she did not like the trio of the Scherzo, "It does not seem to me imposing enough, coming after the scherzo."

On December 29th it was played at one of the Museum concerts in Frankfort.

From the Diary:—

"Thursday, December 21st (1882)
  "I had invited Koning and Müller to come
in, so that we might get to know Brahms' new
trio in C major—Who surprised us at it?—He
himself. He came from Strasburg and is going
to stay with us for Christmas . . . . .
  "December 25th.
  "We tried over the trio, but although I am
delighted with some things in it, I am not really
satisfied with it as a whole, except for the andante,
which is wonderful. It is a pity he does not
always polish his work nor cut out dull passages————.
  "In the evening when my pupils came and
we lit up the tree I was quite carried out of myself. They were all very merry—Brahms was in
the best of humors".

At the concert the new F major string quintet
was enthusiastically received, the piano trio not so
well. "It is a pity that Brahms plays more and more
abominably—it is now nothing but thump, bang and
scrabble."

Earlier in the diary we find an allusion to the be-
ginnings of a trio which was probably this one, and
also to another in E flat, which was never published.

  "Berchtesgaden, September 13, 1880 [her 61st
birthday]
  "Johannes was in a particularly nice and
friendly mood, so that I was really able to enjoy
his visit. He played me the first movements of
two new trios, of which I liked the one in E flat
major best."

Both trios are also referred to in a letter from Billroth to Brahms in June of the same year.

The first movement of the C major trio is grandly and boldly planned, in the spirit of Beethoven. The rather involved chromatic passage immediately following the complete statement of the principal theme, as well as the later theme for the piano in G major, are the kind that have given him his reputation for obscurity. If you like Brahms, you like them. The little second theme in the piano with its delicate triplet accompaniment, its weird beginning and surprisingly simple denouement, is one of those which only he could write. It is interesting to compare it with the second theme (in the piano) in the first movement of the clarinet trio (Op. 114). The coda with its rolling piano figure, the accent first up and then down, and then its bold modulations, brings us back to a triumphant statement of the opening theme.

The second movement, a theme and variations, is the most interesting and enduring, with its haunting old Scotch ♩♩. (Compare the C major horn theme in the First Symphony, the second upward jerking theme in the finale of the F minor piano quintet, and the last movement of the G major sextet). Observe also its ingenious combinations of rhythm and its delightful ending, with the extra long bar just before the close. Note particularly how in the harmonization of the sequence before the return of the opening phrase of the theme, Brahms gives us the D sharp, a momentary modulation to E minor, one of the rich linings which makes his counterpoint and developments so warm.

It is difficult to appreciate either the beauty or the ingenuity of the scherzo merely by listening to it played at speed. One must study it bar by bar. It is also difficult to understand how Frau Schumann thought the trio "not imposing enough". Perhaps Brahms changed it after she wrote thus.

The last movement does not purport to be so important, merely jolly, allegro giocoso. In Eugenie Schumann's Memoirs she tells how, whenever Brahms went to the piano to practice, he began by pressing down his two little fingers at the top and bottom of the piano, followed by a rush of arpeggios in contrary motion. Hence, perhaps, the piano figure in this movement.

SONATA IN E MINOR, FOR PIANO AND CELLO, OP. 38

This was the first of Brahms' published Sonatas for piano and another instrument. First came the three sonatas for piano solo, Op. 1, 2 and 5, (1853) then this cello sonata, Op. 38 (1865), then the G major violin sonata, Op. 78 (1879) then the F major cello and the A major violin sonatas, Op. 99 and 100 (summer of 1886), then the third violin sonata, Op. 108, (1888) and last the two clarinet sonatas in 1894.

There is apparently no record of any other cello sonatas lost or destroyed, as in the case of the early violin sonatas, although a duet for cello and piano which he had composed under the name Karl Würth, was played by him in public when he was but eighteen.

This E minor sonata, which was composed in 1865, was dedicated to Brahms' friend, Josef Gansbacker, "esteemed as a teacher of singing and feared as a cellist". Gansbacker had been the moving spirit in Brahms' election as conductor of the Singacademie, and had also procured for Brahms a number of Schubert manuscripts, including the Wanderer, which he prized very highly, and in gratitude for which he dedicated the Sonata, and also himself played it with Gansbacker for their friends. In the course of this performance Brahms played so loud that the worthy Josef complained that he could not hear his cello at all—"Lucky for you, too", growled Brahms, and let the piano rage on.

Gansbacker was the lover and teacher of the phenomenal singer, Marie Wilt, who sang the soprano solo in the Requiem under Brahms. She was so enormous that their friends used to discuss a "voyage around the Wilt in eighty days".

From Frau Schumann (then age 71) to Brahms, March 2, 1890:

> "I had invited a few people to my house yesterday and Hausmann, [cellist of the Joachim quartet] who is here, had promised to play your E minor Sonata with me; but owing to a severe cough I had to put them off the day before, for talking was too painful for me. As I could play, however, I begged Hausmann to come alone for a little while with his cello. And so yesterday we played your Sonata, and I have not had such unsullied bliss for a long time. He played the Sonata beautifully, and I had practiced it well. It is really too magnificent."

The E minor Sonata, although the first of the two cello sonatas, is more comfortable for the cello than the second. It begins with a beautiful long singing theme starting with the three notes of the E minor triad. The second theme contains three of Brahms' "visiting cards", the momentary adaptation of a 3/4 rhythm to a 4/4 bar, the dovetailing of the voices to fill the bar with eight successive quavers, and, (at the end of the statement of the second theme and before the beautiful passage in B major) an instance of the use of two of the three members of the triad. If the sonata were in D minor, Kalbeck and the rest would here hail another F. A. F.

The *Allegretto quasi Minuetto* is one of the movements which it would seem impossible not to enjoy at once. The growth of the theme of the Trio out of that of the Minuet is also typical of Brahms. The third movement is a glorious fugue. Miss May warns against taking it too fast. As she is sparing in such comments, she may have heard it from Brahms when she was his pupil at Lichtenthal in 1871 during Frau Schumann's absence on tour.

QUINTET IN F MAJOR FOR STRINGS—OP. 88

It is extraordinary that this quintet, with its clear and compact structure, and its wealth of beautiful warm, care-free music, is not oftener heard. While this may be partly due to the necessity of the extra viola, the piano quintet, which also calls for an outsider, is given ten times to one of either this quintet or its later companion in G major. Nor is its neglect due to lack of appreciation by the public. It was enthusiastically received from the beginning both in Europe and in England and has grown in popularity ever since.

The F major Quintet was composed at Ischl during the early summer of 1882. Specht says that it was intended as a congratulation on the betrothal of Brahms' friend Ignaz Brüll. Perhaps it was merely coincident therewith.

On July 27, 1882, Brahms wrote Elizabet von Herzogenberg, "I am sending you a little ditty", enclosing the manuscript, hoping to "earn another letter", and asking its return on the 1st. She sent it back on the 2nd and on August 6th wrote him a long letter about the first three movements, with copious extracts from the music (all from memory, as there are frequent minor inaccuracies). While we may infer that the fair Elizabet was showing off, we may nevertheless marvel at an amateur pianist who could thus master a work for strings in so short a time. Specht is sure that Brahms was in love with her all the time, He first met her as a pupil in Vienna, before she married Heinrich, and unaccountably turned her back to her former teacher after a few weeks, possibly through fear of falling in love with her.

At the same time that he sent the quintet to Elizabet, he sent the C major trio to Frau Schumann with a note that he had done "something else that is better", referring apparently to the quintet.

At Christmas 1892, Brahms came to Frankfurt for the first performance of this quintet and the C major trio (see supra p 78).

> "Dec. 24th. A nice pleasant festival—made all the nicer by Brahms' friendly humour . . . We ended the evening with champagne.
>
> Dec. 25th. Practice of the quintet, as yesterday. The first and second movements are magnificent, but the 3rd (and last) does not appeal to me much.
>
> Dec. 29th. Quartet evening. Brahms quintet was enthusiastically received,—it really is a magnificent work—— * * "

The fresh and joyous mood which this work inspires is reflected in its nickname "Fruhlings Quintett". Like the B major trio, the B flat sextet and the A major Violin Sonata, it starts off at once with a lovely tune, simple as a folk-song, friendly from the beginning, in the same mood as the Beethoven F major quartet Op. 59, No. 1. The second theme, with its slow triplet quarter-notes against the 4/4 quarter notes of the second viola and the eighths of the first violin, is unmistakable Brahms.

As with the later A major Violin Sonata, the second movement combines the usual Andante and Scherzo (Siciliano) in one movement. The last movement is a glorious big fugue. It is again amusing to compare Niemann's analysis of it (p 285) with that of Specht. The former calls the fugue the "crown of this work",—"Joyous, wildly excited and full of Dionysiac ecstasy", * * "a wild transport of exultation,—while still allowing its place to the enchanting, pleasantly musing and melodious second theme—and then at the close gradually leads us back to a peaceful evening mood—all so irresistible and natural"——. Specht, on the other hand, says of it that, though vigorous, it "no longer speaks of emotion, but only of the composer's pleasure in a contrapuntal feat"— which he says recalls the exercises exchanged with Joachim. The second subject, although "a dark red bud, gloriously unfolded," "wearily sheds its petals after only four bars." He suggests that Brahms intended this severe movement to convey to the "young" bridegroom (Ignaz Brüll) an "exhortation not to be content with warbling like a singing bird, but to strengthen his own music by a solid foundation of workmanship in the manner of Bach."

That two such learned experts who apparently agree on the "clarity" of this work, so radically disagree in interpreting its spirit, may encourage the less learned of us each to find his own interpretation, with the assurance that even Brahms himself was not conscious of all the beauties which his genius put into his music, or of a fraction of the pictures, whether of sunshine or of storm, which they may suggest.

QUARTET IN A MAJOR FOR PIANO, VIOLIN, VIOLA & CELLO, OP. 26

This quartet, like its companion in G Minor, already discussed, is attributable to the period of intensive discipline following the Schumann article in 1853. Niemann dates it from 1856, but it was certainly completed at Frau Rosing's house at Hamm, near Hamburg, where Brahms lodged in 1860–2. "Contrary to his custom", Brahms played Dietrich "some sketches" from it there in October, 1861. The first reference to it in the Schumann letters is hers of July 29, 1861, (already quoted supra p. 74), when she had apparently received the A Major Scherzo at the same time as the whole of the G Minor quartet. She remarks on the similarity of the second theme to a passage in Robert's string quartet, and says:—"I think it is the same with this piece as with many others of yours—one only gets to like it when one knows it thoroughly and has heard it often."

On July 10, 1863, however, she writes from Baden:—

"Both Kirchner and I are fascinated by your quartet—I have played it at two parties at my house, the last time with excellent players, Jean Becker, Jaquart (cellist) and Koning, an excellent viola player. Rubinstein heard it on both occasions, but does not yet understand it; however, Lachner from Mannheim, was very appreciative (which means a good deal for an old Kapellmeister). Then there were Levi and lastly Kirchner, who did not lose a note even the first time. To my mind, it is a wonderful work, except for a few passages which seem to me harsh or dull (e. g. the close of the trio in the scherzo), and we have greatly enjoyed it. I must confess you were right after all, it is more beautiful than the G Minor, and finer altogether; the first movement is far more finished."

After the favorable reception in Vienna of the G Minor piano quartet in October, 1862, (see supra p. 73) Brahms took courage to give a concert of his own, at which the A Major quartet headed the program, followed by his Handel Variations (Op. 23) and numbers by Bach and Schumann. Brahms was at his best, sensing the sympathy of the audience. Strangely enough, the Variations were applauded much more enthusiastically than the Quartet, which the critics (Hanslick) thought "dry and flat", "the themes not musically important". Brahms' delight at his success is reflected in his letter home:—

"Dear parents;

"I was very happy yesterday, my concert went quite excellently, much better than I had hoped. After the quartet had been sympathetically received, I had great success as a player. Every number was greatly applauded, I think there was real enthusiasm in the room . . . . .

"I played as freely as though I were sitting at home with friends; one is certainly influenced quite differently by this public than by ours. You should have seen the attention and seen and heard the applause——I am very glad I gave the concert . . . .

"Tell the contents of this letter to Herr Marxsen [his teacher] . . . .

"Did you sit together on Wednesday [his mother's birthday] over the egg punch? Write to me about it and anything else . . . . . .

"How about the photograph of the girl's quartet? Am I not to have it?"

Frau Schumann later writes Brahms repeatedly of the enthusiasm which this quartet evoked when she played it, at Hamburg, Frankfurt, London and other places, though in her diary in 1865 she says:—

"June 10.

"We had Robert's D Minor Trio and Johannes' A Major Quartet, which he played himself and which gave me great pleasure, although my old fears that it will never be generally popular, returned. There are some beautiful things in it."

This quartet, says Colles, is "unique in Brahms' chamber music for the variety of material and for the mastery in knitting it together". The opinion of the experts apparently is, however, that the scherzo and the last movement are unnecessarily drawn out. Both the second theme of the first movement and the opening theme of the scherzo are stated first by the strings without the piano, a device which Brahms used not infrequently. The recapitulation of the second theme and the unusual (for Brahms) chromatics in the coda (just after the familiar thirds and sixths) are noticeable. The Adagio is one of Brahms' great movements. The opening eighth-notes on the strings in unison with the melody of the piano in quarter-notes, give a strange effect,—as if the strings were lost for a moment—as does the presence of the mutes on the strings against the piano *tre corde*. The mysterious piano arpeggios are likened by Fuller-Maitland to a "cold wind blowing over a deserted graveyard;" by Kalbeck to a lovely spring evening

with nightingales in full song.   The little extra en-
largement which Brahms gives the theme in the coda
is a very high spot.   The last two movements are both
cruel to amateur performers.

SONATA FOR CLARINET AND PIANO IN E FLAT MAJOR, OP. 120, No. 2

This Sonata was written as a companion piece to that in F minor which has already been discussed (supra p 61). It is in a less serious vein. The opening theme, with that of the Andantino of the Clarinet Trio, has been criticized by some of Brahms' staunchest adherents as "commonplace". It is neither as noble, as compact, as inevitable or as perpetually fresh as most of Brahms' principal themes. Its treatment, however, is real Brahms, as is the second theme and the delightful coda.

The second movement is marked *allegro appasionata*. It is suggested that a better title would be *allegro energetico*. It boils with explosive energy. This movement is certainly not the work of one who gently floats toward the end of life's stream, mourning a lost love, as Specht would have it.

The last movement is an andante with variations, peculiarly suited to the clarinet. The final variation in E flat minor, *allegro*, with bits of striking rhythmic originality, leads to a coda in E flat major, *tranquillo*. The rhythm in the six bars following the two upward diminished sevenths is bewildering until we see that each phrase begins on the last beat of the bar and carries over through the third beat of the next, without any steadying voice to hold the beat, requiring great artistry in performance to keep the hearers orientated.

QUINTET IN G MAJOR FOR STRINGS, OP. 111

It is noticable that so many of Brahms' chamber works go in pairs, the one direct and joyous, the second serious, compact and overpowering. Whether this merely followed his development or was the deliberate result of his appreciation of contrast, we cannot be sure; perhaps both. The two clarinet sonatas, the two string quartets, op. 51, the two sextets, the two string quintets, the two overtures, op. 80 and 81, the Schicksalslied op. 54, and the Triumphlied, op. 55, the C major and C minor trios (op. 87 and 101) and the A major and D minor violin sonatas (op. 100 and 108).

It is idle to attempt to choose any of Brahms' chamber works as the greatest. For one it may be the piano quintet, for another the horn trio, for a third the G major sextet or quintet, for a fourth the clarinet quintet, for others one of the sonatas or string or piano quartets or other works. Each is entitled and welcome to his own best love. All Brahms' critics and friends, however, unite in agreeing that this G major quintet is one of his greatest works. It teems with lovely and ever fresh melodies. In it Brahms has attained absolute command of form without the least strain.

"His new quintet," Frau Schumann wrote in her diary, "is exquisite".

Elizabet von Herzogenberg to Brahms (Oct. 9, 1890):

> "The 'old' quintet, the F major, affected me so powerfully again recently that the new one only found a footing with difficulty (old friends are the fondest!); but my heart soon surrendered

to the new-comer, and is prepared to admit its possibly greater beauty and benignity, its riper, sweeter vintage. Yet why compare them, when they are so eminently worthy to stand side by side!" * * * *

"The very opening charmed me * * * How it meets one's comprehension half way by its exquisite proportions, its compactness! How clear is the frame-work, thanks to the absence of everything superfluous, and how perfectly each part fulfils its allotted function! * * * I could kiss the second subject [of the finale] and all the sweet tangle after it. It is so pretty the first time it comes, clever the second, and irresistible after the development (which one wishes had been longer) where it comes twisting again upon D. * * * The person who invented it all cannot but have felt very light-hearted. One feels you must have been celebrating—say your thirtieth birthday!"

"It is almost with consternation", says Specht, "that one sees the sexagenarian inventing more richly, more easily, naturally and captivatingly, than he had ever done in his youth."

"Of all the composer's works," says Niemann, "the second String Quintet is the one which most revels in tonal effect, the most passionate, the freshest, and the most deeply inspired by nature."

Kalbeck maintains that this quintet was originated in a Fifth Symphony, which Brahms began but never finished. It was one of Brahms' own favorites. After a rehearsal some one once suggested to him, as a title for it "Brahms on the Prater", to which he instantly replied, with a twinkle in his eye "Youve hit it! and all the pretty girls there, eh?"

On January 2, 1897, three months before Brahms' death, Joachim and his colleagues gave a public performance of this quintet in Vienna. Though Brahms was so weakened and emaciated with his disease (cancer of the liver) that he could scarcely go out, he attended both the rehearsal in Joachim's rooms, and also the public performance. Four months later Joachim, who also considered this one of his friend's "most beautiful works" wrote Ernst Rudorff:

> "I often think sadly of the last pleasure it was in our power to give him and to which he responded with unusual gentleness. I have never heard him express his gratitude so warmly as after listening to his G major Quintet; he seemed almost satisfied with his work."

The opening of the first movement sweeps all before it, as the cello soars up out of the shimmer of the others. This passage gave rise to much argument and discussion on the part of Joachim and his colleagues, and also of the members of the Rosé quartet (which gave it its first performance in Vienna in November 1890). The cellists, Hummer in the Rosé group and Hausmann in the Joachim, (each famous for his big tone) had trouble in surmounting the *forte* of the rest, and they suggested subduing the latter, but Brahms was obdurate. After the performance in Berlin in December, Joachim wrote Brahms, in answer to the latter's request for his opinion:—

> "And now the desired report as to the opening passage. After trying it in various ways, we came back to your original version, except for a slight modification of the forte from the end of the second bar, increasing the tone later."

At this first performance, in deference to the irrepressible enthusiasm, Joachim, contrary to his practice, repeated the allegretto, and thereafter always had to do so to each succeeding audience.

"The opening of the development," wrote Elizabet von Herzogenberg after the Berlin performance, "is indescribably fine, with its powerful Bach-like progressions: F, E flat, D flat, C, and G, F, E flat, D. How Joachim and Hausmann looked at each other there, and what a blissful moment it was for us all."

The Adagio, which Joachim so admired, stands beside those in the horn trio, the A major and C minor piano quartets, the C major piano trio, the D minor violin sonata, the F major string quintet, and the clarinet trio and quintet, as representing his most profound and enduring slow movements.

The finale is another instance of the influence on Brahms of the Hungarian folk music, ending with a *frisca*. Niemann calls attention to the position of this quintet between the two groups of gypsy songs, Op. 103 and 112.

QUARTET IN A MINOR FOR STRINGS, OP. 51, No. 2

In July 1867, Joachim wrote Clara Schumann that "Brahms has promised to send me some string quartets", and in June 1869, she records that "Johannes brought me two exquisite movements for a quartet, the first and last", the latter "höchst geist- und schwungvoll; the first would require some change to suit my taste; perhaps he will alter it, since he himself does not seem entirely satisfied with it." The two finished quartets (Op. 51) were not forthcoming until four years later, when she writes Joachim (August 29, 1873) that she has received "two quartettes of the greatest importance."

Both quartets are dedicated to Billroth, the distinguished Viennese surgeon and Brahms' most intimate amateur musical friend, in whose beautiful music room many of his chamber works had their first performance. As has been noted, Kalbeck's theory was that the first four notes of the A minor quartet represent a combination of Joachim's motto F A E with Brahms' F A F (here A F A) and hence a veiled dedication to Joachim. Although all the biographers seem to accept this theory, none of them purports to advance it on the authority of either Brahms or Joachim. In October 1873, Brahms wrote Joachim telling of his pleasure at hearing that Joachim was to play the A minor in public and saying: "Neither of them were really meant for your violin". * * *

Apropos of these quartets, Billroth writes in January, 1875:

"Brahms desires very moderate tempi throughout as otherwise, owing to the frequent harmonic changes, the music cannot become clear".

Brahms was very open minded about his tempi, and for this reason omitted metronome marks, believing that the performers should have considerable latitude to suit their mood. Henschel records a most interesting talk with him on this subject.

Of the two, the A minor quartet is the most pleasant and inviting. Specht characterizes the first movement as "one of the most ingratiating pieces ever written by Brahms, who here forgets all his asperities". Elsewhere, however, he describes it as "a work that might be written by a Schubert who has read and painfully experienced Schopenhauer". The characteristic slow triplets and the prevalence of mixed rythms mark this movement as unmistakably Brahms. The Andante and Minuet are both gracious, although not (for Brahms) extraordinary, the Minuet foreshadowing the Liebeslieder Waltzes, (Op. 52). The finale, with its displaced syncopations, and its thoroughly characteristic coda, is true Brahms.

SONATA IN F MAJOR, FOR PIANO AND CELLO, OP. 99

"Are you expecting Hausmann?" Brahms inquired carelessly of his friend, Frau Fellinger, on his return from Thun to Vienna in the fall of 1886. Suspecting that something lay behind the question, she at once telegraphed the great cellist, and on the very night of his arrival the new F Major Sonata was tried at her house, and again later at a large party given by Billroth on the day before its public performance at Hausmann's concert on November 24th.

An amusing reference is found in Elizabet von Herzogenberg's comments on this sonata (after playing it with Hausmann on his return) to Brahms' habit of grunting uncouth noises into his beard as he played—audible to the first half dozen rows in concert halls:

"So far I have been most thrilled by the first movement. It is so masterly in its compression, so torrentlike in its progress, so terse in the development, while the extension of the first subject on its return comes as the greatest surprise. I don't need to tell you how we enjoyed the soft, melodious Adagio, particularly the exquisite return to F sharp major, which sounds so beautiful. I should like to hear you play the essentially vigorous Scherzo. Indeed, I always hear you snorting and puffing away at it—for no one else will ever play it just to my mind. It must be agitated without being hurried, *legato* in spite of its unrest and impetus."

Niemann says that the F Major Sonata was written especially for Hausmann, having in view the unique features of his cello playing. He apparently had a tone so big and luminous that it could rise, even here, above the piano fortissimo, or, as in the G major quintet, above the other four strings. It is a tremendously difficult work to play, but a most satisfactory one when mastered. One need not, without question, accept Niemann's assurance that the sonata "speaks in accents of suffering passion rather than of soft lamentation", or agree that "it does not, on the whole, quite come up to the level of the first" (E minor, Op. 38). Miss May says that in it "the emotions are reached through intellectual imagination," whatever that means.

The first movement, with its seething and heaving tremolo on the piano and its sudden outcries from the cello, anticipates the mood of the G major Quintet. Comment has been made on the fact that the Adagio leaps to the remote key of F sharp major. One of Haydn's piano sonatas (No. I Vol. 1 of Schirmer Ed.), however, does the same thing, the first and last movements being in the key of E flat major, and the Adagio in E major.

QUINTET IN F MINOR, FOR PIANO AND STRINGS, OP. 34

Except for the violin sonatas, the piano quintet is the best known and most frequently heard of all Brahms' chamber-music. It would be difficult to choose any more representative work.

Its evolution illustrates clearly Brahms' unerring instinct for and mastery of the proper and effective use of musical material. He has left us no symphonies for the Violin alone, like the Bach Chaconne.

The quintet was first written for five strings, with two celli, then recast as a sonata for the piano (which, fortunately, we still have as Op. 34a) and finally reduced to its present form for piano and four strings.

It was composed, as a string quintet, during the summer of 1862, at Munster and Hamm, and the first three movements sent in manuscript to Frau Schumann. On September 3rd, she writes from Lucerne:

"I hardly know how to tell you calmly what a joy your quintet is to me. I have played it through several times, and my heart is full of it. Your things seem to grow more and more splendid, more and more glorious. What strength, what richness, there is in the first movement, and how the first theme takes hold of one at once! How beautifully it is scored for the instruments! I can see them bowing. You ought to send yourself with each of your compositions so that one could discuss every bar properly with you * * * * *. At the close that dreamy passage and then the accelerando and the wild passionate ending—I cannot tell you how it moves me and how it has taken hold of me. And what an adagio! How rapturously it sings and rings from beginning to

end! I keep on beginning it over again, and
wished it would never stop. I like the Scherzo,
too, very much, only the trio seems to me a little
short, and when is the last movement coming?"

Joachim was "hoping" to get the manuscript in
October from Brahms, who had taken it with him on
his first visit to Vienna.

The "last movement" came to Frau Schumann in
December and delighted her. "It sums up the whole
thing", she writes on December 18th, "and is full of
go * * * In fact, it is quite masterly. If only I
could hear it, for playing it at the piano is so trying
and unsatisfactory. Did you hear it in Vienna?"

Whether or not he asked Hellmesberger and his
colleagues to play the quintet for him at Vienna "in
November" (as Frau Schumann wrote Joachim he
hoped to arrange) is not clear. Brahms certainly
had misgivings about the work—(the strings being
insufficiently sonorous to give expression to its great
material). He took it with him on his visit to Dietrich
at Oldenburg at Christmas, and on May 1, when he
went to visit Joachim in Hanover to meet "Jusef's"
fiancée, Amalie Weiss, he asked Joachim to try it
over for him. On May 26th, 1863, Joachim writes
Frau Schumann:

"I was able to have his quintet played for
him. It is a great pity that the general effect of
this piece, in spite of so much that is remarkable
in it, should be unsatisfactory, and I was glad
that Johannes, on hearing it himself, wished to
alter it. A man of his strong character cannot
accept anything on hearsay."

A year later, on March 10, 1864, she writes
Brahms:—

"I cannot quite understand what you have
written me about your Quintet. Did you pro-
duce it and was it a frost? And did you, on that
account, turn it into a Duet? If this is so, you
cannot have been satisfied with it yourself in its
original form or pleased with the way it sounded.
Could you not have altered it quite easily and
yet have left it as a Quintet? Surely there were
only a few passages which did not sound well and
much of it at least gave the impression of being
a quartet?"

On April 4 Brahms wrote her from Vienna (where
he was directing the Singacademie) of the plans for
an extra concert on April 17th of "only Brahms", at
which they were to do the Ave Maria, the Marienchor,
the motets (Op. 29) and the solo quartets (Op. 31)
the B flat sextet "and finally my sonata for two pianos
which I shall play with Carl Tausig."

While the concert as a whole was a great success,
the sonata, strange to say, fell flat. On July 19, Frau
Schumann wrote from Baden thanking him "for the
duet" which she had "practiced hard for two whole
days."

"I had wanted to play it with Rubenstein,
and, as there was only one part written out, I
had to play it from your first score, which was
really not easy. However, I was richly rewarded
by the pleasure I found in playing it, and Rubenstein too, grew quite enthusiastic about it."

She then goes on to say that, while it delights
her, there are some "small things" she would like to

suggest, and asks that he do not print it "until we have played it here a few times. And then perhaps one thing or another may occur to you yourself."

Three days later, after she had studied the sonata further, she again wrote:

"After the happy hours which I have spent with Levi over your Sonata, dear Johannes, I must add something about it which I have very much at heart. The work is on a wonderfully grand scale, its skillful combinations are interesting throughout, it is masterly from every point of view, but—it is not a sonata, but a work whose ideas you might—and must—scatter, as from a horn of plenty, over an entire orchestra. A host of beautiful thoughts are lost on the piano, and are recognisable only by a musician, the public would never enjoy them at all. The very first time I played it, I felt as if it were a work arranged for the piano, but I thought I was prejudiced and so I did not say anything. Levi, however, said the same thing, very decidedly, without my having said a word. If only I could point out all the passages which delight me—one, the change into 6/8 time, seems to me more striking than words can say. I felt after it as if I had been reading a great tragedy. But please, dear Johannes, for this once take my advice and recast it. If you do not feel fresh enough to do so now, lay it by for a year and then take it up again. Surely, the work will come to give you great pleasure."

What with the Vienna failure and Frau Schumann's advice, Brahms apparently went to work at once again to recast the work and on November 3rd, she writes acknowledging the "glorious quintet", which Levi and David (the Carlsruhe Kapellmeister and Concertmeister) "sit copying out as if nailed to their seats and Levi tells me how wonderful the instrumentation is." On November 10th she again writes to tell of their delight in playing it several times. "You have made it all exquisite."

During Brahms stay at Baden near Frau Schumann in July and August 1864, they had played the sonata privately for Princess Anna of Hesse, who had been much impressed with its beauty. Brahms accordingly asked her permission to dedicate it to her, and on its completion as a piano quintet, and dedication also in this form, Frau Schumann, ever on the lookout, managed to seize the opportunity to suggest that the Princess buy, and donate to Brahms, the manuscript of Mozart's G minor symphony, then apparently offered for sale. "The moment was so propitious that she commanded me to buy it then and there; you will realize with what joy I did this when you see it. * * * How triumphant you must have felt over the erasures". (Frau Schumann here alludes to Brahms' habit of rubbing out his mistakes with his wet thumb).

While we all rejoice in having the Piano Quintet, we also rejoice that the Sonata has been preserved to us (Op. 34a) since there is no more glorious or satisfactory work for two pianos.

A small volume might easily be written on the musical structure of this quintet. A few points of interest stand out.

The first movement, which dominates the whole work, shows us the "heaven-storming Johannes", now guided by a master-hand. The wealth of material and imaginative power which pervades it defy analysis. The opening commands instant attention, heightened by the dramatic pause on the dominant, followed by the rushing piano and the hammer blows from the strings, which precede the full statement of the first theme. Particularly noticable is the way in which the piano suggests the second theme in the cadence preceding it. Throughout the work we find constant illustrations of Brahms' power of fertilizing his themes and extracting from them new material, giving to his works an extraordinary coherence and solidity. Miss May suggests an enlightening analogy between this quality in Brahms' music and the secret force that governs all natural organic development.

The first movement contains four independent theme groups. The rhythms in this movement are of themselves a subject for an essay. Its conclusion, from the *poco sostenuto* for the strings alone, with the glorious awakening and triumphant end, gives one of Brahms' most precious moments.

The Andante (would that we could hear it for the five strings too) is filled with Brahms "visiting cards", thirds and sixths, rich modulating linings in the sequences, cross-rhythms in slow triplets, veiled mystery preceding refreshing clarity, and ending in the favorite plagal cadence with the F flat in the viola.

The scherzo, boiling from the beginning and growing in momentum until it tumbles gloriously down to the C major chord at the end (really the dominant minor ninth of F minor leading to the last movement) is, with the final presto, the most exciting work to play that can be imagined. The stately trio, with its parenthetical asides for the piano, its baffling rhythms and its sequence in Brahms' favorite suspended sevenths,—pungent as the wood-smells on a cloudless Canadian morning,—gives to the riotous scherzo an effective foil.

The finale opens brooding, with slow triplets and ever mounting figures leading to the real movement about whose interpretation Niemann and Specht so radically disagree (supra p. 26). An interesting feature of this movement is the way in which the Allegro, after the full statement, begins all over again. The 21 bars (Tempo I) constituting the little interlude to give us breath, before the final 6/8 presto, make one of the most sublime spots in all chamber music.

QUARTET IN B FLAT MAJOR, FOR STRINGS, OP. 67

The Third String Quartet, often called the Pastoral from the "hunting calls" of the first theme and in the *doppio movimento*, is the most joyous of the three. In this form alone, Brahms has made the later work the least sombre.

Although not apparently completed or given even to Frau Schumann and Joachim until May 1876, it was composed during the spring of 1875 at Ziegelhausen on the Neckar, where Brahms was staying with Hanno, the portrait painter, and where he was very happy. "I am delightfully lodged," he wrote, "and pass my time delightfully". Here, also, he finished the third (C minor) piano quartet, which the biographers consider "so sinister" and "feverishly agitated". (Query, whether music is more likely to reflect the composer's present mood than to be a means of escape from it; compare Mozart's clarinet quintet, wholly joyous music, written when he was sick, hopelessly in debt, just after Constanze announced another prospective baby).

On May 22nd, Joachim wrote Brahms:

"You have never written better chamber music than the D minor movement and the Finale, the former full of enchantment and romance, the latter full of grace and sincerity of feeling."

From the Diary:

"Berlin, May 23rd (1876). Such a surprise yesterday!—a new quartet by Brahms (string quartet in Bb major) which Joachim played to me. He and his quartet had come to play it

through, as well as some other new works. I
had told him of the quartet's existence and he
sent for it secretly. That was Joachim all over!"

On the same day she wrote:

"Dearest Johannes:—

I must send you a word of thanks, today
after the happy hours we spent over your quartet,
yesterday and the day before. Joachim set to
work at it at once, so that it grew into an exquisite clearness—it is not easy either to understand
or to play. The third and fourth movements are
my special favorites, and I really do not know
which I delight in most, the sweet tones of the
viola in the third, or that charming theme and
the way it is interwoven. The theme is too
fascinating for words, with its delightful, mocking
conclusion. I hope Joachim will play it again
this week."

From the Diary:

"June 4th. Matinee at Joachim's. Brahms
F minor quintet which gives me more pleasure
each time I hear it . . . . a piece in which I
revel from beginning to end. Brahms Bb major
quartet. The 1st, 3rd and 4th movements are
beautiful. The adagio (2nd movement) seems to
me not to have enough weight for Brahms."

This quartet was dedicated to Brahms' friend,
Dr. Engelmann, who beside being professor of Physi-
ology at Utrecht, was a good amateur cellist and
husband of Emma Brandes the pianist. Brahms
wrote him in August 1876:

"I am about to give birth to another string
quartet and shall need the help of a medical man

as in the case of the two others". (dedicated to
Dr. Billroth). "This time I do not think forceps
will be necessary". (Brahms had travailed with
his two first quartets for more than seven years).

"I need not now," Dr. Engelmann wrote in reply,
"worry so much about immortality!".

In October Brahms wrote to Simrock complaining
good-naturedly of the delay in publication and saying:

> "For a fee I am asking only a paltry 15,000
> marks. From this amount, being a natural born
> scoundrel, you will at once deduct 3,000 marks;
> for delay 1,500; for additional delay in the four-
> hand arrangement 1,500; because there are only
> two flats in the key, 750; for cigars, tobacco,
> eau de cologne etc. 2250; by flim-flamming the
> accounts you will skin me out of 3000 more;
> and you having already lent me 600, leaves a
> balance to me of 2400; * * * To this I must
> add; because the Adagio is such a short one 45;
> because I am sending the MSS for each move-
> ment 7½ pf—30; for sketches of the tender
> movement, 2 Gulden."

The quartet revels in changes and combinations
of rhythm. 6/8 and 2/4, 4/4 and 5/4, and finally
2/4 and 6/8.

The third movement, *agitato*, was a particular
favorite with Brahms, who told Henschel (at Sassnitz
on the island of Rugen, where they spent the summer
of 1876 together) that he considered this movement
"the most amorous, affectionate thing he had written".
Specht, however, who finds passion and love in fugues
and motets, does not like it. In this movement the

viola takes the prominent part, its three companions being muted throughout.

In October 1876, after having heard Joachim and his colleagues play the quartet in private, Brahms wrote Joachim a most interesting letter containing specific suggestions regarding the tempi. He points out that the passage in the Scherzo (at letter B in the Eulenberg score) after the retard "is not marked *scherzando*".

> "There should be no change" he goes on, "in the mood of the music and the indication *poco a poco in tempo primo* (up to about the 3rd bar) must not be neglected. You will excuse me, as you probably did not credit me with such finesse. I always imagine my own renderings to be very rough, but in writing, I have all sorts of refinement and delicacy in my mind. * * * Are you entirely ignoring my request that you should alter some of the notes in the more difficult passages, especially in the first movement? The necessity for fingering is proof of bad writing" * * *

The final variation in the last movement brings back the opening theme of the first, as in the G major violin sonata and in the clarinet quintet, both later works.

TRIO IN E FLAT MAJOR FOR PIANO, VIOLIN AND WALD-HORN, OP. 40

Each of the four movements is a master-piece. Any one of them may properly be chosen as the favorite, or even one on one day, another the next. The most critical examination from one end to the other, will disclose no weak spot. It is hard to find a serious musician who does not like The Horn Trio. There is but one such work.

Brahms himself played the horn when a boy in Hamburg and was always fond of it. It has often, with him, the decisive word, as in the Requiem, the beautiful three part chorus (Op. 17) for women with two horns and harp, the D major Serenade, the opening of the Second Symphony, the B flat concerto, and, best of all, its radiant entry with the Swiss shepherd's call in the finale of the First Symphony.

There had been a splendid horn player, August Cordes, at Detmold, during Brahms' three years stay there.

When he wrote this Trio at Baden in the summer of 1865, Brahms had few models for the unusual combination of piano, violin and horn, there being no previous horn trio and no sonatas for horn and piano other than the Beethoven Op. 17, in F major (usually played by the cello) and unknown sonatas by Lessel and Bernsdorf.

Brahms intended this work for the wald-horn and not for the ventil horn, believing that the natural notes of the former have a fuller quality than those produced by the valves. "If", he says in a letter to Richard Heuberger, "the performer is not obliged by

the stopped notes to play softly, the piano and violin
are not obliged to adapt themselves to him and the
tone is rough from the beginning."

After the first private performance at Carlsrühe
on December 7th, 1865, Brahms wrote to his friend
Dietrich, director of the orchestra at Oldenburg,
apropos of his proposed visit for a concert:

> "For a quartet evening I can with good
> conscience recommend my Horn trio, and your
> horn player would do me a great favor if he
> would do like the Carlsruhe man and practice
> the French [natural] horn for some weeks before-
> hand, so as to be able to play it on that."

Westermann did so practice on the hand horn
and the public performance was apparently a great
success. Of it Dietrich says in his Reminiscences:

> "Every one was deeply impressed by the
> horn trio and by its originality and romanticism.
> Some years later, when we were wandering to-
> gether on the wooded heights above Baden-Baden,
> Brahms showed me the spot where the theme of
> the first movement of this work came into his
> mind."
> "I was walking along one morning", he said,
> "and as I came to this spot the sun shone out
> and with it this theme". (Dietrich to Miss May).

An interesting item in the history of this work
was its performance at Basle on March 26, 1867, with
Brahms and violinist Abel, by Hans Richter, later
the great Wagner conductor, who began his career as
a hornist.

Although Kleinicke at Vienna played it on the wald-horn, Frau Schumann's hornist at Frankfort could not be persuaded to do so.

"I had meant to write to you from Leipsic," she writes Brahms from Coblenz on December 22, 1866, "the day after the quartet evening when I played your horn trio, but I left Cologne the next morning and all these last days were one wild rush. We had studied your trio (I had begged it from Simrock) very well, and the horn player was excellent. I do not think he spluttered once, and that says a great deal; though it is true that he played on a ventil horn. He would not be induced to try a wald-horn. The Scherzo was applauded most energetically, and next to that, the last movement, which went as if fired from a pistol."

Little can be said to supplement the music of this work. It is one of those in which Brahms rose above himself to that universal expression which is the rare privilege of the great alone. A few points in its structure are interesting.

An important feature of all Brahms chamber music is his choice of themes adapted to each of the instruments participating, and not suitable merely for one of them. This is especially noticeable in the themes of the Horn Trio, which sound equally well on horn, violin and piano, a most difficult problem, solved so simply that the original difficulty is wholly forgotten.

The first movement is not, as usual, in sonata form, but in that of the old *divertimenti*, with no development section. Almost at once Brahms' favorite cross-rhythms make their appearance, triplets in 6/8 against the syncopated 4/4 in the first section, and seconds against the triplets in the 9/8 (animato). Still another rhythmic surprise comes later in the piano part with the syncopated triplets just before the G minor section preceding the return to the first theme. The coda of this movement is pure Brahms, as is that of the Adagio.

Particularly noticeable in the Scherzo are the sudden injection of one, two or more bars of 2/4 rhythm interrupting the galloping 3/4. Also the startling modulations, enharmonic changes and augmented sixths (again in the last movement). When in the Trio of the Scherzo (written in the unusual key of A flat minor and reminiscent of the similar movement in the first piano sonata Op. 1) Brahms gives the direction *molto* meno allegro, he means *molto*.

He who is searching for pure beauty, direct from the creator of all things, need look no farther than the two solo bars for the horn announcing the second theme of the Adagio; nor is there, in all music, a more beautiful passage than that where this theme in the violin combines with the first theme in the piano, to express a musical thought obviously different from each of the two. Another immortal moment is where the piano part (two bars before the restatement of the second theme by the others) slips in the B double flat. This modulation to the sub-dominant just at the end, while one of the effects taught to all students of composition, is used by Brahms with supreme mastery. We find it again at the end of the Andante of the D minor violin sonata (C natural in the D

major) and still again, (although less striking) in the
last movement of the G major sextet.

Frau Schumann's description of the last movement ("shot from a pistol") does not mean that it
must be hurried. Again we have the baffling rhythms,
3/4 against the 6/8. No music could be more satisfying than the triumphant re-entry of the first theme
on the violin, after the retard and accel. to tempo by
the horn and piano in their dialogue at the end of the
little development section.

When, (as usual) a competent horn player is not
available, the horn part may be played on the viola
or cello. While one critic prefers the viola, to most
the cello is the more satisfactory, the viola tone not
being big enough to fill up the passages intended for
the horn, which can always be heard pianissimo.

QUARTET IN C MINOR, FOR PIANO AND STRINGS, OP. 60

Miss May rates this Third Piano Quartet as "decidedly below its glorious companions, Op. 25 and 26", and as much the least popular of the three, although "the easiest to grasp at first hearing". Colles, on the other hand, describes it as "one of the best loved of Brahms' works". Specht and Niemann both consider it one of his strongest and most moving compositions, although the latter says that it is "esteemed and admired rather than beloved and popular". Miss May, who preferred the original B major trio to the revised version, apparently had an ineradicable prejudice in favor of the works written before she studied with Brahms in 1871. Both her conclusions would seem open to question. Certainly there is nothing "inferior" about this quartet. The Andante and Scherzo rank with his best, and the second theme in the first movement is one of his most precious.

The quartet has a long history. The greater part of it unquestionably dates back to the middle 50's when Brahms was in the midst of the turmoil of soul over Schumann's illness and death and his struggle with himself over "Clara". The origin of the Scherzo, however, the most tumultuous and explosive of the four movements, dates behind that, since it is said to be the offspring of the Scherzo written by Brahms for the Sonata to surprise Joachim in October 1853, for which Schumann (under the caption F. A. E.) wrote the first movement and Dietrich the last, and which Joachim gave to the Brahms Gesellschaft for publication in 1906. An examination of the early Scherzo

would not seem to bear out the statement by the
biographers that that of the Quartet was a "revision"
of it. They are rather two different Scherzos from the
same hand, the first a beginner (the trio of the old
Scherzo is terrible) the second a master. Apparently
the first movement of the C minor quartet, (as well as
the Adagio), was conceived in the middle 50s and laid
aside to be taken up again in 1873–4, and finished, with
the last movement, in 1875. When Brahms played
Dieters the sketch of the first movement in 1868,
Brahms said: "Now think of a man who is just going
to shoot himself, because there is nothing left for him
to do," explaining further that while this feeling was
not intended consciously to be portrayed by the music,
the music was the outcome of such feelings at the time
it was conceived.

In his letter to Simrock when he sent it for publication:

> "This Quartet is both old and new, and so
> the whole fellow is good for nothing. * * *
> furthermore, you may place a picture on the
> title page, namely, a head—with a pistol in front
> of it. This will give you some idea of the music.
> I shall send you a photograph of myself for the
> purpose! You may also make use of a blue
> frock-coat, a yellow waist-coat and top boots, as
> you appear to be fond of color prints."

It is because of the latter allusion that this is
sometimes called the Werther Quartet.

It was probably this Quartet which he "had
ready to show" Joachim and which he tried over in
private in 1856.

Specht calls the beautiful Adagio his "farewell to Clara", Widmann "Brahms' avowal of love". Kalbeck tells us that the first movement was originally in the key of C sharp minor. In Frau Schumann's diary for October 18th, 1856, is the following:

"Johannes has finished his Concerto. We have played it several times on two pianos. He has composed a wonderfully beautiful Adagio for his C sharp minor quartet—full of tenderness." "Tuesday 21st. Johannes left. I went to the station with him—as I came back I felt as if I were returning from a funeral."

On August 5, 1859, she also writes "And what about the quartet? I heard that you played it with Reimers at Frau Peterson's". The reference to Johannes' playing implies a piano quartet.

Although the experts all thus connect this quartet conclusively with Frau Schumann and the stormy days of 1855–56, it is puzzling to explain her own complacency with regard to it when she heard it in its completed form in 1875. In July of that year we find her writing to Brahms:

"With heartfelt content I look back on our pleasant afternoon with you, and your music has been a real refreshment to me—I ought to have pleasures of this sort frequently, as I realize only too well.

I have been thinking about the quartet a great deal, and the last three movements have taken quite hold of me, but—if I may say so— the first does not seem to me on the same level, it has not the same freshness—though there is freshness in the first theme. I should have liked to hear it once more, that I might be quite clear

why it did not make me enthusiastic. Could
not you—who often carry a movement in your
head for ever so long—manage to alter it, or to
write a new movement? You have already
proved many a time how easily you can slip into
the same train of thought again, and to what
splendid effect. Forgive me, perhaps all this is
quite stupid.''

If the quartet had in fact sprung directly from her
relations with Brahms, might we not expect her to
have known of this in 1856, and to have remembered
it in 1875? Women never forget these things.

An interesting feature of the structure of the first
movement is the reservation of the full restatement of
the first subject for the coda. The second subject
section of this movement consists of a little set of variations on the first piano theme.

The splendid Scherzo and Adagio have already
been referred to. The former is as exciting as the
Scherzo in the Piano Quintet and the latter, with its
delightful rhythmic tangles, is equally fascinating.
Specht thinks that the piano figure which pervades the
last movement contains an intentional allusion to
"Fate knocks at the door". Interesting if true. When
some stupid pedant called Brahms' attention to the
similarity between this piano figure and the opening
of the Mendelssohn C minor trio, he said:—"Das
sieht jeder narr." While he was spending the summer
with Henschel at Sassnitz in 1876 Brahms referred to
this chance and specious resemblance, pointing out
that what with Mendelssohn constituted the theme
itself, was with him merely an accompanying figure.

TRIO IN C MINOR, FOR PIANO, VIOLIN AND CELLO, OP. 101

This trio was the third of the triology written at Thun during the happy summer of 1886. It is universally considered one of his most powerful works. "No previous work of Johannes," says Clara of it in her diary, "has so completely carried me away."

"Oct. 27th. Rehearsal of Brahms' trio. I owe hours of bliss to this work."

"Oct. 28th. The trio (Brahms') went magnificently. We had worked at it well together and I played it with the greatest enthusiasm. The audience was quite carried away; we had to repeat the second movement and they wanted the third as well * *

"We were all together in the evening when Stockhausen came in. There arose a great dispute over Handel, and Woldemar got quite excited. Brahms was silent at first, and then became rude. Stockhausen, when he had nothing left to say, began to sing, thus silencing all opposition."

"The C minor trio", says Specht, "is a self-portrait if ever Brahms created one, amazingly concentrated—an extract of his whole nature compressed into thirty-six pages. In the first bar the principal theme is hurled down in chords like thunderbolts, and we can see the master at the piano, throwing back his head with a mighty jerk, with flashing eyes, a grey-blond mane and a full awe-inspiring beard, and we seem to hear his curious grunting and panting as he plays."

A striking resemblance has been noted between the opening of this trio and that of the Third Grieg

Violin Sonata in the same key. Each work was completed before the other was published, and so the resemblance was a clear coincidence on both sides.

The Andante, a duologue between the piano and the strings, goes back to the folk song for its rhythm, one bar 3/4 with two 2/4, while the second subject varies between 9/8 and 6/8.

The second (muted) movement (presto) Frau Herzogenberg considered the "pearl among them all." "Its ghost like figures are so tangible in their beauty."

Of this trio she wrote after her receipt of the manuscript at the end of 1886:

> "Few things, I imagine, have ever been so perfectly proportioned as this trio, which is so passionate and so controlled, so powerful and so lovable, so terse and so eloquent. I suspect your feelings as you wrote the last bar were very much those of Heinrich der Vogler in his prayer 'Thou gavest me a goodly catch, for which I thank thee, Lord.'"

"I wager", Joachim wrote to Brahms in July, 1887, "that not even you have often written anything more beautiful than the Trio in C minor."

SONATA IN D MINOR, FOR VIOLIN AND PIANO, OP. 108

In a letter to Frau Schumann on October 19th, 1888, Brahms spoke of "a little violin sonata" and on November 2nd wrote to her:

"The violin sonata which I mentioned the other day I have sent to the Herzogenbergs, and I have received such an unexpectedly kind letter about it, that I am wondering whether it might not please you too. * * * Forgive me for not having sent you the sonata first, but you will never believe my chief reason for not having done so. The truth is that I can never do a piece the credit of believing that it will please anybody. I feel the same about this one * * * If the sonata does not please you when you play it through, do not try it with Joachim, but send it back to me."

The above, as well as the similar depreciation of the revised B major trio, was not prompted by any false modesty, nor, it is believed, by Brahms' failure to appreciate the soundness of his work, but from the fact that his ideals constantly outstripped any possible realization of them. Nothing that he ever could do came up to what he would do, and so long as he tested his productions merely by his own conceptions he was dissatisfied. Only when his friends judged them by their standards, did they appear masterpieces.

Frau Schumann promptly sent for the sonata, and though unable to play it herself owing to neuralgia, she heard it from her daughter Elise and Koning and was overjoyed with it.

"What a wonderfully beautiful thing you
have once more given us * * *. I marvelled at
the way everything is interwoven, like fragrant
tendrils of a vine. I loved very much indeed the
third movement which is like a beautiful girl
sweetly frolicking with her lover—then suddenly
in the middle of it all, a flash of deep passion,
only to make way for sweet dalliance once more.
But what a melancholy atmosphere pervades the
whole! The last movement is glorious * * *"

By December 8th her hand allowed her to play
and she gave a "party for musicians", at which she
and Koning played. "I enjoyed the sonata enor-
mously * * * they were all enthusiastic."

"Jan. 7. Brahms arrived * * * On the 8th
B tried the sonata with Heermann. He played
it as I have always imagined it, except that he
took the adagio slower"

Soon after that Joachim came and she had another
"party of musicians" at which she and Joachim played
the sonata "twice running."

Johannes to Clara: (then in her seventy-first
year):

"Vienna, Nov. 1889 * * * The thought of
my D minor sonata wandering along gently and
dreamily under your fingers is too pretty and
pleasant. I actually laid it on my desk and in
my thought went gently stealing through the
organ-point shrubbery with you. You always
at my side, and I know no greater happiness than
when I sit by your side, or, as now, walk beside
you."

Clara (aged 74) to Johannes:

"Frankfort, Feb. 1, 1894. We also had Joachim with us for an evening and he played me a quartet by Robert and then played your third sonata with me. That was a joy such as one seldom has! In the first movement, with its singing harmonies melting into each other, I had constantly the feeling that I was floating on the clouds. I cannot tell you how I love this sonata; every movement of it—who knows whether it is not the last time I shall ever play it!"

Johannes to Clara—Vienna, February 8th.

"How delighted I am when you write as kindly about my music as you have this time about my third violin sonata; I went straight away and took it up tenderly and played it to myself."

In view of the foregoing from Frau Schumann, who with Joachim understood Brahms' music as perhaps no one else ever will, what matters it that Miss May and Specht dismiss this glorious sonata with a few curt words! Neimann, at any rate, thinks it the greatest of the three, but that it contains "more reflection than spontaneity."

The "letter from the Herzogenbergs", which Brahms mentions in the first letter quoted, was really from Elizabet and contains an extraordinarily discerning appreciation of the work, too long to quote in full (see pp. 360–362 of the Herzogenberg Letters). She describes vividly how the manuscript arrived early in the morning and how they rushed half-dressed to awake Amanda Röntgen (violinist), Elizabet and Heinrich fighting to play the piano part.

"Our eyes flew from bar to bar, our zeal and delight grew from page to page, our fingers tackled every difficulty with such success that I hardly knew myself" * * *

"At the opening of the development we quite held our breath. How new it is, with that exquisite pedal note absorbing everything! How our surprise and delight grew and grew as the A showed no sign of giving way, but held its own through all that glorious tissue woven above it! How my left thumb revelled in the pressure it had to exert! And that F sharp minor on that Proteus A and the gradual ebbing until the theme's subdued return—*molto legato*. O, my friend, that was indeed one of your moments." * * *

"What delights me so in this sonata is its wonderful unity. The four movements are so unmistakably members of one family. One purpose dominates them; one color scheme embraces them all; yet their vitality finds expression in various ways." * * *

"I rejoice to find the Adagio undisturbed by any middle part * * * How comical (in the best sense, for one laughs for pleasure) is the Presto in its breathless hurry, and how rich in every line * * * The finale has in the highest degree the one quality essential to a finale—an irresistible impetus. It tears along like Aurora's steeds in the glorious picture."

"One day," Eugenie Schumann writes in her Memoirs, "he [Brahms] played the piano part in his violin sonata in D Minor at our house. Mamma used to say that there was one bit, marked 'tranquillo' at the end of the third movement, where one walked on eggs. Marie and I were most anxious to hear how he would manage to get safely across. When it came, he took the tranquillo so excessively slowly that nothing could happen. We smiled at each other. 'There he goes, tip-toeing over the eggs', we thought".

Elizabet von Herzogenberg suggested that the violin chords at the opening of the Scherzo be taken pizzicato. Brahms adopted this in the repetition, but made a special legato mark against the violin chords in the beginning. Of the finale, she says:

> "The more I play the Finale, the more hopelessly do I fall in love with it. I hardly know anything else that tears along with such spirit * * * How glorious it must be to feel that it has lost none of its original power in the process of development from that first conception to its present elaborately worked out form!"

QUINTET, IN B MINOR, FOR CLARINET AND STRINGS, OP. 115

There is believed to be no more profound, masterly and lastingly enjoyable work of chamber-music, than this quintet. Were it alone, it would make Brahms immortal

The occasion for its composition has been described in the discussion of the Clarinet Trio (supra p 45), written at the same time. With the Trio it was privately performed at Meiningen by Mühlfeld, Joachim, Hausmann and two members of the orchestra in November, 1891, and publicly in Berlin in December. During the rehearsals Brahms wrote Hanslick that the Adagio was played "as long and as often as the clarinetist could hold out". At the concert this movement was repeated in deference to the enthusiasm which would have had all four movements a second time. Immediately after the Berlin performance, Joachim wrote (in English) to Sir Charles Villiers-Stanford, to arrange for a performance in England of the Quintet, "one of the sublimest things he ever wrote". Brahms, he says, will give the manuscript only on condition that they engage Mühlfeld "a stupendous fellow", there being "too much Gypsy-stile" in it for an English clarinetist. Thanks to the generosity of an English admirer (Alfred Behrens) who had offered to finance the first English performance of the German Requiem and who later bequeathed Brahms £1000, Mühlfeld was engaged and two performances were given in London with progressive enthusiasm by both performers and audience, since when it has been received with both reverence and affection whenever and wherever adequately heard. While the clarinet part may be played on the viola, no one who has heard it only in this form can fully understand its beauty. It is really a different work.

One wonders how anyone with understanding (such as G. B. Shaw, a chronic scoffer at Brahms) knowing this work, can assert that Brahms' music is all "harsh" and "unmelodious". From all four movements the loveliest melodies are continuously bursting.

Somewhat less incomprehensible, but misleading nevertheless, is the tendency on the part of the appreciative to call it a sort of swansong, "flooded with the last red glow of an artist's evening." While it may possibly signify "quiet and painfully agitated resignation" or "gentle regret" to those looking for regret and resignation, for others it may have a wholly different message. What Brahms was thinking when he made it we will never know, nor does it matter. The music speaks to each in his own language.

In a short article in The Musical Times for July 1, 1926, Mrs. Carl Derenburg (Ilona Eibenschutz) a pupil of Clara Schumann, who as a young girl had often been present at Brahms' visits to her in Frankfort, vividly describes a performance of this quintet:

> "Mühlfeld (Clarinetist) came to Ischl for one day to visit Brahms and played Brahms' Clarinet Quintet with the Kneisel Quartet. This was the most wonderful performance I ever heard. It took place at Kneisel's house, the audience consisting of Brahms, Herr and Frau Steinbach, Herr and Frau Nikisch, and myself. Mühlfeld played marvellously on his clarinet, and when they had finished playing this heavenly

work, we were all so moved that nobody found a
word to say. But Nikisch fell on his knees before Brahms, and that exactly expressed our
feelings."

Thoreau says that the singer "can easily move
us to tears or laughter, but who is he who can com-
municate a pure morning joy?" Thoreau never heard
this quintet, nor the opening of the G major violin
sonata, nor the beginning of the G major sextet, nor
Feldeinsamkeit, nor the Andante of the Second Symphony.

The Quintet as a whole epitomizes the treatment
of noble musical ideas with perfect balance and unity.
The first movement opens with Brahms' favorite
thirds and throughout is filled with his individuality.
One never tires of it and new beauties appear at each
new hearing. Even Joachim required some time to
get "quite used to the C sharp and F major" in the
development section.

The Adagio is unique in music, both in variety
and depth of the material and in mastery of construc-
tion. Its opening is a perfect example of Brahms'
rhythmic originality and complication. The clarinet
sings a beautiful quiet tune in simple 3/4 time, while
below it each of the other four instruments weaves its
separate path in a wholly distinct rhythm from all
the others,—a great bird soaring above a busy city
with the people going their separate ways below.
Then comes the famous middle section where the clarinet is allowed to show off all that he can do, saying
something, however, all the while. After each bravura

passage is finished by the clarinetist, the first violin quietly explains what he has really been talking about.

The third movement is again in the "morning joy" mood, with a *presto* middle section furnishing a striking contrast. The last movement consists of variations on a musical idea, done in Brahms' incomparable variation style. Particularly interesting is the music-box variation; also the change to 6/8 time and the reintroduction of the theme and mood from the first movement. Best of all are the last lovely descending notes of the clarinet, repeated from the end of the first movement.

"Thus falls a star, and thus it is extinguished."